AF522582

SMASH IT!

Alison Edgar MBE is the MD of Sales Coaching Solutions and The Entrepreneur's Godmother. Voted one of the UK's Top 10 Business Advisers, Alison works with SME's, start-ups, micros and entrepreneurs to help them grow their business through effective sales. As a sales coach, Alison works with businesses around her Four Key Pillars of Sales methodology, to help business owners and sales teams gain essential sales skills and knowledge and implement strategies and processes enabling them to sell more of their fantastic products and services. Through training, coaching, workshops and online courses, Alison has worked with hundreds of businesses, including some of the UK's most promising entrepreneurs featured on *Dragon's Den* and *The Apprentice*.

SMASH IT!

The Art of Getting What You Want

ALISON EDGAR

RUPA

Published by
Rupa Publications India Pvt. Ltd 2025
7/16, Ansari Road, Daryaganj
New Delhi 110002

Sales centres:
Bengaluru Chennai
Hyderabad Jaipur Kathmandu
Kolkata Mumbai Prayagraj

Copyright © Alison Edgar MBE 2025
This edition of Smash It! The Art of Getting What You Want is published by arrangement with Rethink Press.

The views and opinions expressed in this book are the author's own and the facts are as reported by her which have been verified to the extent possible, and the publishers are not in any way liable for the same.

All rights reserved.
No part of this publication may be reproduced, transmitted, or stored in a retrieval system, in any form or by any means, electronic, mechanical, photocopying, recording or otherwise, without the prior permission of the publisher.

P-ISBN: 978-93-5702-809-7
E-ISBN: 978-93-5702-673-4

First impression 2025

10 9 8 7 6 5 4 3 2 1

The moral right of the author has been asserted.

Printed in India

This book is sold subject to the condition that it shall not, by way of trade or otherwise, be lent, resold, hired out, or otherwise circulated, without the publisher's prior consent, in any form of binding or cover other than that in which it is published.

CONTENTS

INTRODUCTION

Have you ever looked at someone and thought they've got it all? Perhaps they've got the perfect relationship, the big house, the dream job, or maybe it's all that and more? Whatever it is, it's something you've always wanted but try as you might you never seem to get it. Or you might not have a clue what you want. You're at a crossroads, you feel lost and you're waiting for that eureka moment, where all your questions are answered and the path ahead becomes clear.

It seems every time you look around you are surrounded by people who are achieving amazing things. You are sick of watching people boasting about their new house, toned abs, hot relationship, fancy holidays, perfect family, purring the engine of their new car or yapping on about their well-paid job. Why does it always seem to happen to them, not you? You just never seem to catch a break.

Social media frustrates the hell out of you. In an Instagram world, it's easy to compare yourself to other people. Social snooping is at an all-time high. The world has access to engagement rings as soon as they have been slipped on fingers, we can see newborn babies seconds after they have been delivered, we can even have a Facebook Watch Party and feel like we are in the middle of someone's life.

Do you just want to shout STOP!? You crave the answers but up till now you just can't seem to find them! You wish there was a book that has everything in one place, that would give you the tools you need to crack the code to get what you want.

Well, congratulations, you have found it! My book is the one you have been waiting for, here's what it will do for you:

- You can only achieve your goals when you know what they are. This book helps you identify what you really want and gives you a clear plan of how to get it.

- 92% of people struggle to reach their goals *(Inc. Magazine, 2018)* because they don't know why they set them to begin with. This book increases your likelihood of achievement by helping you to understand what drives and motivates you.
- Teach you how to identify and alter your mindset to help you build mental strength, tenacity and stay positive, even through difficult times.
- Help you become self-aware; understanding how to utilise your superpowers to get what you want, whilst acknowledging your vulnerabilities to prevent them from tripping you up.
- Sometimes getting what you want involves other people, this book teaches you the power of persuasion to collaborate, cooperate and communicate with others effectively in order to achieve your goals and get them in your corner.
- You will learn the techniques to take action and stop procrastinating, giving you the courage to start and the confidence to finish.

Let's be clear at this stage, my name is not Genie and I do not live in a lamp. If your expectation is that you are going to make a wish and everything you ever wanted from the million-dollar bank balance to the body of a supermodel will land in your lap in the next five minutes, you are very much mistaken. This handbook is full of techniques and skills to enable you to get what YOU want in your life. To get those things, YOU are going to have to take action, YOU will have to put in the work to make it happen.

I am notorious for getting what I want, but it doesn't always happen the first time, every time. I have to practise what I teach and keep going until I make it happen. Patience and hard work are key ingredients to getting where you want to go. If you are not prepared to commit to either, maybe it's not a book you need to help you, it's a magic wand!

Firstly, I would not describe myself as a self-help guru or life coach. Controversially, I'm not a believer in manifestation and abundance. I honestly believe it's all skills and hard work. It is important you have a vision, but you need to grab it with both hands, not sit and wait for it to come to you. But hey, if it works for you, that's fantastic.

Secondly, if you're looking for a highly academic book, this is not the one for you. Some of the techniques I use are based on tried and tested theories, models and fundamental psychology, others I have created myself. It's the combination of all that gets the results. Throughout this book, I'll be featuring case studies of individuals that have used my teachings to get exactly what they want. This may be through workshops, coaching or them simply just reading my first book. This isn't to promote myself; this is simply so that you can see how real people have implemented my techniques to get what they want.

If I had to compare this book to something it would be Baz Luhrmann's (1999) *Everybody's Free (To Wear Sunscreen),* this is a long-term favourite of mine and has been a great provider of sage advice throughout the years. If you have absolutely no clue what I'm talking about, I suggest you jump on YouTube and give it a listen. In the words of Baz Lurhmann: "The long-term benefits of sunscreen have been proved by scientists, whereas the rest of my advice has no basis more reliable than my own meandering experience" – well that and the evidential true stories of people who have used my methods to get what they want.

Be in the 8%

According to *Inc. magazine (2018*), only 8% of people reach their goals, that leaves 92% who are struggling to get there. With hundreds and thousands of personal development and self-help books on the shelves, how can this still be the case?

In my opinion, some of the books are written around the individual's personal struggle and whilst they make great inspiration, they don't actually help YOU get anywhere. Others fill you with promises of life-changing formulas and techniques, but when push comes to shove, they are too complicated to follow or not sustainable, working better in theory than in real life. Then you have the ones that work, the ones that make everything make sense and elevate you into the 8%.

The SMASH IT! method can do this for you. I know it can because I have seen it work time and time again, not just in my own life but in that of my clients, friends and family. When it comes to getting what you want, there are only two real obstacles getting in your way – you and other people. My method gives you everything you need to remove obstacles from your path and SMASH your goals. It is simple and easy to follow, but best of all it is realistic. You can use it every single day, it doesn't require hundreds of hours of your time. You don't need any magical equipment or to join any exclusive groups. All you need is this book and the determination to get what YOU want.

Some of the theories in this book you may be familiar with, especially if you are an avid watcher of TED Talks. It's the combination of having it all in one place and breaking it down into bite-sized digestible chunks that makes the magic happen!

Writing things down helps you to remember and recall information, so throughout the book there will be tasks for you to complete. Book formats have changed, and some people will be reading on a Kindle or even listening to the audio version. As you won't be able to write in the task boxes, I've created an interactive app which includes all of the tasks in digital format alongside a whole bunch of other funky tools to keep you accountable. I recommend everybody downloads this to help keep you on track whilst you create your master plan.

Head to www.smashitbook.com/app to download or scan the QR code at the start of the book.

The Calling

I know this may sound like the title of a scary horror film, but it's how I feel about writing my books. My debut book *Secrets of Successful Sales* launched in March 2018 and was created to help entrepreneurs and salespeople achieve better results. The book has been an overwhelming success but something totally unexpected happened. I was inundated with messages from people who love it and have used my techniques to help them get what they want, not only in business but in their personal lives too.

People have used my methods to give them the confidence to do things they only ever dreamed of, like securing a promotion, new careers and life pathways, resolve conflict with family or friends, improve their work-life balance, better deals when buying a house, more money when selling a car, losing weight and organising their finances. The changes have been outstanding and you will hear from them through the book as they tell their own stories in their own words to help you.

So you see, I didn't want to write a personal development book, this book has called me to write it. I have a successful business and had no desire to change direction, but if you are not in business or sales you would never have picked up my first book as you would not think it's relevant to you, but look at you now, you are reading this because it can help you get what YOU want.

Due to demand, writing this book was always on the cards but the time frame was stepped up by the COVID-19 pandemic. Since the start of 2020 the world has been turned upside down, things we took for granted like hugging our family or friends, popping to the shops, going to work in the office or venturing on holiday could not happen. Even now as I type these words it seems impossible that the whole world was brought to a halt by a virus. Through no fault of their own people have had their lives desecrated, they have lost loved ones, businesses and jobs and I could see my social media and messages were awash with despair and people's hopes were fading.

2021 sees the vaccine delivered to help eradicate the virus, but what about the devastation that COVID-19 has left in its wake? How do you rebuild confidence, positivity and reduce anxiety and fear? This book is the shot in the arm you need to rebuild your life in the aftermath of a terrible experience.

The techniques I teach work and by working your way through the book they will give you the skills you need to SMASH IT!

Here we go again!

"Can you hear me, Mrs Edgar? Mrs Edgar, can you hear me? We need your consent to operate. Can you hear me, Mrs Edgar? If you can hear me just nod. We need you to understand during the operation we may have to remove some parts of your body which means you will not be able to have any more children. Can you hear me? Do you understand? Do you give us permission to operate?"

It sounded like a Saturday night edition of *Casualty*, the long-standing BBC TV hospital drama show, which always has some medical emergency going on. But it wasn't, it was real, and it was happening to me. These words were being spoken directly to me but they were coming at the end of a stream of other words and noises which were alien and I was struggling to comprehend what they meant and what was going on.

It started with the loud overbearing buzzing noise, coming from somewhere I couldn't identify, mixed with the crying of a baby, a newborn baby. I wish someone would stop the noise. It was *very* annoying. All I wanted to do was sleep, but the noise and crying were bringing me back from drifting off into my cosy place, that and the dizzy, nauseous feeling.

The next thing I heard was the shoes, not like the nice clip-clop of happy dancing shoes but the tread of rubber-soled trainers, squeaking against the floor. Not just one pair either, lots of pairs, it reminded me of a primary school PE class.

Then there are the running and breathing sounds, why are they running, what on earth is going on? Then AHHHHHH the pain is intense, the runners with the heavy breathing are pushing me on something, but why? What are they doing? What the hell had I just hit to cause the pain?

'Bing', what's going on now, I hear a lift, what am I doing in the lift? Ahhhhh I've hit something again. I'm still struggling to figure out what is going on but it seems to be that I'm being pushed on a bed. Am I on one of those charity bed pushes? Why am I being thrown around on a bed, like I'm on a scene from *Wacky Races?* Then it starts to become clearer, I'm remembering, I know where I am, I'm in the hospital and I've just had my baby Kieran. Kieran, Kieran, *where is Kieran*?

I can see things but I can't speak, I can't ask them what's going on as my mouth just doesn't seem to be working. Maybe it's a dream, I think I'm dozing back off again. Nice! When I wake up I'll be all wrapped up in my own bed and duvet. But I can't get back to sleep, the people around me are so noisy and they are poking me, I want to shout "Shut up and STOP POKING ME," but I can't, the words won't come out of my mouth. There are more of them now, I can't really see them, but they are all wearing the same blue tunics and caps. One of the pokers shouts, "We can't get a line in, the pressure is too low," and from the back of the room someone shouts, "Put a central line in, she has started shutting down, we have to go to the theatre NOW."

The familiar female voice asks again. "Mrs Edgar, can you hear me? We need your permission to operate, please can you nod." I don't really remember much after that but I must have nodded, as when I woke up I was in the post-operative section of the hospital.

If you are one of those who struggle with blood and guts, don't worry I'll spare you the gory details. To cut a long story short, it turns out that after delivering Kieran by emergency caesarean section at the end of a 24-hour labour, the stitches hadn't held and I had been haemorrhaging internally for many, many hours, which had gone undetected. It was only when I said I was feeling queasy they realised my blood pressure was too low to be detected by the monitor, and it sent everyone into a frenzy.

According to the UK National Health Service Blood and Transplant team, on average a woman has 10 pints of blood in her body. Without getting too detailed, losing blood is natural during childbirth. There are four different stages, ranging from stage 1 where you lose 10-15% of your blood when you can feel a little faint and light-headed to stage 4 where you lose over 40% of your blood volume. This type of haemorrhage is so severe it requires immediate and major resuscitative help, or else the strain on the body's circulatory system will be too great to survive. The heart will no longer be able to maintain blood pressure and circulation, so organs fail and patients slip into a comatose state preceding death.

My medical records show on 6th December 2000 I needed a nine-pint transfusion, so the fact I lived to tell the tale is something of a miracle and reflects in most part the skills of the team at the Royal United Hospital in Bath and a thank you to all the fantastic men and women who give their time to give blood to save people like me.

If I were you at this stage, I would be re-reading the cover of the book again to make sure you had bought the right one… What does this have to do with The Art of Getting What YOU Want?

Well, as I mentioned, this book is the follow-up to my debut book *Secrets of Successful Sales.*

I compare writing that book in a lot of ways to the birth of Kieran, not that I nearly died but it was quite a traumatic experience, and looking back retrospectively there were many times when I was close to putting the manuscript in the bin.

As a dyslexic author, getting the words from my head to my fingers and on to paper is never an easy task; not only do the letters dance around, but sometimes I don't have the faintest idea how to spell the words I want to use, what hope does the grammar checker have? Human nature tells us we do the things we like to do first, and for me, writing is never at the top of my list, I would much rather be chatting or faffing around on social media.

Again with the help of my co-conspirator Kiya and a lot of hard work, we managed to create *Secrets of Successful Sales*. She helped me pull the words out of my head and get them on paper, I would write, she would edit, we would read, we would laugh, I would cry, but eventually we created something which we hoped people would like. But then comes the fear… what if we have spent all this time and no one reads it? Then the second fear, what if we have spent all this time and they read it and think it is rubbish, eeeekkkk, that was the biggest nightmare.

A key factor I omitted to tell you about the operation after Kieran's birth was that despite giving my permission, the surgeons managed to perform the surgery without completing a hysterectomy, which gave me the option to have more children. It is the words of my consultant which ring in my ears as I type; lots of people who have had traumatic first births put off having more children because they are scared, they worry it will happen again, sometimes they wait so long that it's impossible to have more children. Their fear holds them back from getting the family they wanted. It would have been easy for that to happen to me, given all that I had gone through, but I knew I wanted to have two children. So I looked forward and put the trauma behind me. Success! Seventeen months later, with the help of my family, friends and doctors, we welcomed the lovely Connor to the world.

I compare the journey of writing my books to having my family. In the words of the consultant, it would be easy for me to put off writing another book because writing the first one was so difficult, but that's just not me.

Why do I tell you this? Well actually because getting what you want isn't going to be an easy journey. It doesn't have to be about having children but I highlight this because for me it was traumatic; for others, it could be falling off the bike and being afraid to get back on. It doesn't matter what it is or what you're trying to achieve, anything worth having just doesn't come easily. You will slip up, but that's OK as long as you don't give up.

WHAT DO YOU WANT?

That's the million-dollar question!

You might be reading this thinking I know exactly what I want. It seems from the minute you were born you've had your whole life mapped out in front of you, just like that 13-year-old girl who has been planning her wedding down to every detail from the six bridesmaids and 112-piece croquembouche to the sugared almond favours. Or maybe you're more like I was when I started my business, and have never had any goals, in fact, the first thing you think of when you hear the word goal is your favourite football player kicking the ball in the net on a Saturday afternoon.

It's usually at this point when you don't know what you want that you start looking around at others for inspiration. What are my friends doing? What have my colleagues got? What do my neighbours have?

She's going on holiday to the Caribbean, maybe I want that? He's just got a new promotion, maybe I should go for one of those?

Just because Jenny from the block is driving around in her new Jaguar F Pace, or has dropped two dress sizes, doesn't mean this should be your goal, you need to find your own path and reasons why you want it.

Before we go any further, I want you to give me your commitment. I want to STOP you in your tracks, do not compare yourself to others! You are not them, you are YOU!

To understand the importance of this you only have to look at the case of John Landy vs Roger Bannister at the Empire Games Mile in Vancouver, Canada in 1954. I know it was probably before you were born, me too, so let me fill you in on what happened. Back in the day, Landy and Bannister were the top sportsmen in their field, both breaking the four-minute mile record within a few weeks of each other. The race was much anticipated and elevated them into a celebrity status around the world. They were very different types of runners. Landy was a strong, tanned, muscular Aussie. Bannister, a pale, slim Brit, who you may know from his story in the film *Chariots of Fire*.

The Empire Games was their first head to head meeting since 1952. The tension was electric as the world watched with anticipation to see who would take the crown. On paper Landy was the favourite to win, his style was a stronger more 'out front' kind of running. In reality, it was looking like the odds were right, Landy was leading throughout the full race until the very last straight. Seconds before the finish, Landy looked back to see where Bannister was, it was that error which allowed his opponent to overtake him. He was comparing his performance to Bannister and it was his lapse of concentration which cost him the race.

When you concentrate too much on those around you, it's easy to forget about yourself and where you are. Much like Landy, we are all guilty of comparing ourselves to others; in fact, a psychologist called Leon Festinger (1954) developed a whole theory around this very subject called Social Comparison Theory. As humans, we have an innate drive to evaluate ourselves and often we do this by comparing ourselves to others. Just like Landy at the Empire Games Mile, the easiest way to know your position in a race is by comparing yourself to your competitors.

We all compare ourselves to someone else, it's human nature, but in a world of social media self-comparison has become a dangerous obsession. Festinger's theory shows that positivity can come from self-comparison, as those around us can be a great source of motivation and inspiration, showing you that your goals are achievable. I've had many positive role models over the years but it's important to set boundaries and ensure, like Landy, it doesn't stop us from crossing the finish line. Constantly comparing yourself to others can be a kicker, demotivating you and discouraging you from going after what you really want. After all, this isn't the Empire Games we're talking about, it's life and the only person you really should be competing with is yourself.

My mother used to use the saying 'No one knows what goes on behind closed doors'. I think this is more true now than ever before. It's easy for us to watch someone on YouTube or Instagram living their rock star lifestyle and think they've got it all, but what we don't see is what happens when the cameras stop rolling and they have to return the Maserati they hired for an hour and go back to living in their parents' box room. I'm not saying that this is always the case but you never really know what goes on in other people's lives. There's a good chance that while you are looking at them thinking why do they have everything I want?' they are looking at someone else thinking the exact same.

This book is not titled The Art of Getting What Other People Want! This one, my friend, is all about YOU.

To get your creative juices flowing, start writing down some things you want.

In the box, write at least three things you want. This should take you no more than two minutes to complete. Don't worry if you can't think of anything right now, you've got a whole book to help you come up with ideas and you can come back to this at any time.

WHAT DO YOU WANT?

1.

____

____

____

____

2.

____

____

____

____

3.

____

____

____

____

Get SMART

They say the oldies are the goodies and one of my favourite goal-setting frameworks is the SMART method as developed by George Doran in 1981:

SMART = **S**pecific, **M**easurable, **A**ttainable, **R**ealistic, **T**ime-based

Being SMART is key, it's times when we are not that we are more likely to fail or feel unsatisfied when we do achieve. By keeping your goals general, you're keeping yourself in the dark; saying "I want to buy a house" doesn't give you anything real to aim for, all you've done is made a simple statement that you can complete anytime from next week to the next 10 years. When you're SMART your goals become so much clearer and achievable, you can actually visualise the finish line and when you can see it you become more determined to cross it. As the saying goes, when you can see it, you can achieve it.

Specific

Thinking about what you want can be a daunting question, some people just quite literally haven't got a clue. A bit like when I asked my housebound elderly Mum what she wanted me to get for her food shopping and her response would always be, "Something nice!" This made supermarket visits extremely difficult. But her vagueness was not done to be awkward or irritating, it was driven by an overwhelming amount of choice. How did she know what she wanted for dinner next Wednesday when she had just had breakfast on Saturday? This is exactly the same when someone doesn't know what they want. According to an article published by the *Huffington Post* (2017), the top 10 things that people want but just can't seem to get are happiness, money, freedom, peace, joy, balance, fulfilment, confidence, stability and passion.

Did you write any of those words down? What do those things even mean? They are just wishy-washy! They mean nothing at all. Being generic is your enemy, it is a barrier and why you need the help of my book.

Let's take the word stability, it's general and hard to define. For some people, stability may take the shape of buying a home of their own. Putting down roots may be their first step to commitment and could give structure in their life; for others it could mean leaving the house each day and keeping their mental health balanced. But, for this section, let's focus on the property as our example.

The next part of being specific is to work out who is involved in the purchase, are you doing it on your own or with a friend, partner or family member? If others are involved and you are struggling to convince them, you definitely need to read the 'WE thing' section of the book to get them thinking your way!

You need to know why you want to buy the property, maybe you are sick of paying rent and want to have a long-term investment for your future. We will be looking more in depth at WHY later as it's the WHY which keeps you focused on the difficult days.

There are lots of types of houses and flats, in millions of streets throughout the world, you only have to watch the buyers with Kirsty and Phil on *Location, Location, Location* to see how overwhelming it is to get your foot on the property ladder. But having a clear financial picture, accessibility and geographic area will help you be specific and is a great place to start.

For example, I want to buy a two-bedroom flat with my partner, within a three-mile radius of Warbeck Road, Shepherd's Bush, West London because we both work in White City and it means we can walk to work and won't have transport costs. We have a deposit of £50,000 and the mortgage payments per month are £1,600 which fits with our income and outgoings. Our current lease agreements end in May, so we would look to move in then.

Already you can see that the craving for stability has started to become an actionable plan. Being specific and clear helps you be accountable and achieve your goals.

Measureable

If something isn't measurable then you'll never actually know if you achieve it.

In the case of the house, you have to have saved a certain amount every month to have the deposit. That is very measurable as you will see it in your bank balance. You will also know if you find the house of your dreams as you have put a strong geographic radius and time frame of when you want to move in.

Data is very important as it helps you see if you are on track. This is where I think lots of people give up hope; especially at the moment during the pandemic, lots of people will have had their house-buying dreams quashed through no fault of their own. Maybe their savings are depleted, they've lost sources of income or no houses are available in the area.

Measurement can sometimes become daunting and obsessive, especially when it comes to things like weight loss or saving money. Don't look at measurement as a negative, use it as a positive to help keep you on track. Check your progress at regular but spaced-out intervals, and don't beat yourself up about it if you're not making progress as quickly as you'd like. Slow and steady wins the race!

Attainable

In other words, how achievable is the goal you've set for yourself? Banking has come on leaps and bounds and there are amazing apps such as Starling and Monzo which show your disposable income and help you save for the things you want. But what if the mortgage payments are more than your combined salaries? Try as hard as you want, you will not be able to afford it.

You then have choices to make: you either have to find ways to make more money, ie better paid job, secondary income or business, more deposit, or even rethink the geographic location to reduce the house price. You don't have to give up, you just have to adjust your expectations.

Realistic

This is about ensuring the goal you set yourself is not only realistic to you but also works with the other goals you've set yourself. This is what this whole book is about: *The Art of Getting What YOU Want*. It's not the art of getting what your partner wants or even what your mum wants for you. We've spoken already quite a lot about setting your goals around what you want and not just based on what those around you have achieved. Here I want you to consider this even further: sometimes we set goals not because we want something or someone else has got something we think we should have but because somebody else wants it for us. A lot of the time you can get lost really striving for something that you never wanted for yourself.

Let's take a multimillion pound house with a swimming pool for example. I see people put this on their goals all the time, not necessarily because they want it but because their partner does, or they think that they should have it as a status symbol to show the world that they have 'arrived'.

Setting unrealistic goals is another of the reasons people give up; they don't feel they are achieving and feel dejected when they don't happen. It's OK to dream big but you need to have the plan to back it up.

The other part of realistic is making sure your goals work together and not against each other. It's highly likely that you will be working on more than one goal at a time, so it's not really going to work if achieving one goal sets you back on another. For example, you can't set a goal to reduce your hours at work and therefore reduce your salary if your other goal is to save more money to pay for a house deposit. Again, it's setting yourself up for failure, you'll struggle to be able to achieve both goals, so make sure they complement what you are looking to achieve.

Time-based

This is the last component in the SMART formula. Every goal needs a deadline otherwise it will simply go on forever, and you'll never achieve it because you have allowed yourself a lifetime to do it. By putting in a timescale, it keeps you on the track to success and helps you break down your goals into smaller daily or weekly tasks that will help you along the way.

Coming back to the big dreams, like the multimillion pound house, it's OK to have it on your list, but if you are not on the housing ladder at all it would be a long-term goal. The secret is to work backwards. These time frames are specific to your goals. If you're losing weight, your long-term time frame could be around two years. If you're building a multimillion pound property empire, this could take over 20 years so there is really no exact rule of thumb for this. Here's an example:

1. Long-term goals – things that can take up to five+ years to achieve. For example, buying the dream house in the country.

2. Mid-term goals – things that take between 12 months and five years to achieve. For example, buying the Warbeck Road property and renovating to increase value.

3. Short-term goals – things that can be achieved in less than 12 months. For example, saving £2,000 a month towards the deposit.

Time frames aren't an exact science and curveballs are thrown at us all the time. This book was written throughout 2020 and into 2021. Due to the pandemic restrictions, most people will have had to adjust the time frames on their goals. In the example of buying the flat in London, instead of moving out of the rental property in May when the lease expires, there would perhaps be an option to rent until November, meaning the goal is still alive, just postponed. You can even set mini weekly or monthly savings goals to help keep you on track. It's really important to put specific times or it's easy to let things slip and that's how dreams fade and resolutions dissolve.

A time frame helps make your goal measurable; when doing this you should also be reflecting on how achievable your timeframe is, and in turn these both help to make your goal specific and relevant to you. All the components of SMART work together, a bit like one big puzzle that comes together to reveal an image of your potential future!

What did you put in your answers in the previous What Do You Want section? Anything like these?

- Buy or move house
- Start a business
- Learn to drive
- Get a promotion at work
- Gain a new qualification
- Get married or divorced
- Send children to private school
- Start a family
- Take up a new sport
- Learn how to cook
- Find romance

- Lose weight
- Reduce overwhelm

It's important you now revisit the answers, drill down on them to make sure they are all SMART as this will improve your chances of achieving them.

Jot down your goals in the section at the top of the box. In the box next to each letter write your criteria for each step of SMART.

For example: T (Time Based) – I will start the big clean-out of the house on 21st July, at the start of the summer holidays, and complete this by 5th September when the kids go back to school.

If your answers were already SMART, you are already starting to SMASH IT!

This should take you 5-10 minutes.

S	
M	
A	
R	
T	

Vision Boards and Crystal Balls

I'm all for positive thinking. It opens you up to new opportunities which can often result in helping you get what you want. But I think there's a lot more required when it comes to achieving your goals. I think you are doing yourself an injustice if you work your backside off to get what you want and then you let the universe take all the credit. You don't get what you want just by looking into the crystal ball and making a wish. However, I do think having a vision is important, in fact, I would go as far as saying it's imperative to help you achieve. Having something visual keeps you on track during the tough days when you feel your goals are unachievable, it helps you focus and take action.

There are lots of tools you can use to create a SMART vision board, you can go with the tried and tested lick and stick method, or you can jump online and use one of the many free tools available. Some of my favourites are Canva and befunky.com. It doesn't matter how you do it, the important thing is to be specific. Use this exercise to really dig deep and break down those vague terms. For example, if your goal is to go on holiday, find pictures of where you want to go, don't just stick in a random photo of a beach and write the word holiday under it. Every picture on your vision board should have a meaning and a purpose.

Using the property-buying example in the last section, if it was me I would go to Google Earth, find a picture and print it out. Every time I want to make a rash spending decision or have an extra takeaway, the photo of my soon-to-be home would help me control the urge to deviate from the savings plan. If you ever do fall off the path, the main thing is to forgive yourself and get back on it. Don't wait for Monday, next week or next month. Too many people self-sabotage and give up, the vision board is a huge tool in your armoury to bring back your focus.

As I mentioned before, eradicate the fluffy words like happiness, freedom and love from the board. You can't see them, and this is a vision board, not a dictionary. These words are subjective to you. Let's think about success: for some people, success may come in the form of them being the CEO of a Fortune 500 company; for others, it may be to chair the Parent Teachers Association (PTA). There are no right or wrong answers but you need to know what it means to you otherwise you will never achieve it. That's why if you can see it, you can be it.

My 2020 vision board was more or less eradicated by the pandemic. I had planned to speak at 10 international conferences around the world, one of which included The European Commission in Belgium, but the world shut. Not only was international travel cancelled but so were live events. I'm not going to lie, my first reaction was, "Holy Moly, what am I going to do with this goal now?" It is easy to get dejected when things don't go the way you want. But I still want to speak at the events as planned, I just have to adjust my time frame to 2021 or even 2022. But with every negative there is a positive, you just have to find it. My positive was that it gave me more free time to write this book.

Another one of my goals was to go from couch to running a half marathon, so I had a photo of me with my running medal on my board, it reminds me of the indescribable feeling I had when I completed my first 5K race. It also keeps me motivated on the cold wet days when I can't bear the thought of putting on my trainers and running gear. Had I just written the word fitness on my board instead of the photo, I'd never feel motivated because it doesn't mean anything. The photo is powerful, resonates with my senses and gives me the oomph to get up and go. Without travel, lockdown gave me more time to exercise and train; you can imagine the feeling when I did my half marathon, I was like the cat that got the cream.

It's your turn now, take your goals and use the tools I mentioned and create your SMART Vision Board.

For this task you can create your vision board in whichever way works best for you, whether that's creating a graphic on Canva or Photoshop or grabbing your glue stick and coloured pens. This one's at your discretion.

What's Stopping YOU?

From my experience with clients, it is normal for them to move into the 'Ah but…' phase. What I mean by that is they start to look for excuses as to why they cannot achieve their goals. It's like a protection mechanism to secure them against failure.

I know COVID-19 will be used as a reason lots of people have not reached their goals yet. For example, if your goal was to travel to Australia for a holiday in December, but the country is in lockdown and not accepting international visitors, it would be *very* easy to blame the virus, the government, the rule breakers or super spreaders. This is an 'Ah but…' to what is going on in the world. You can't control the situation but you can control how you deal with it. Blaming external forces will only eat you up and lead to frustration; you cannot influence the government lockdown rules, but you can influence how you react to it, and in the example of my speaking engagement, you can still visit Australia in December, just not the December you planned.

Sometimes there are workarounds to still achieve a win-win result. Over the last 12 months the virtual world has become normal to most people with hours being spent on Zoom, Teams and Skype. Although live events have been cancelled, virtual ones have been booming. Sometimes it's not about adjusting time frames, you can change the parameters; for example, I took part in an international event in

Bahrain, but by negotiating with the organiser instead of being there physically, I spoke virtually so I still achieved the desired outcome.

The rule of thumb: if you can converse, you can convince.

You see there are only two hurdles that we all face that stop us from getting what we want:

1. Yourself
2. Other people

YOU are one of the biggest things that holds you back. Don't worry, it happens to the best of us. It's not intentional, it just happens, life gets in the way, confidence takes a knock and suddenly the world doesn't seem to quite fall at your feet in the same way as it did when you were a child. As we get older we get more responsible and things just don't come as easily as we all wish they did. I think fearing failure has a lot to do with this. You only have to look at ice rinks all over the world. Novice five-year-olds embrace falling because they realise when they fall they will learn what not to do and it will improve their skating techniques. Their 55-year-old counterparts refuse to let go of the barriers at the edge in case they fall over and injure themselves. But if you don't let go you will *never* experience the magical feeling of gliding on the ice. To make things happen for yourself I need you to think like a child.

This is where I am here to help. The first part of this book focuses solely on YOU. I call this the 'ME thing', everything that you have direct control over. You need to understand yourself and overcome the internal walls that you have built. Together we are going to look at the WHY behind your goals, help you understand your mindset and how to adapt it, as well as identify your behaviour and the superpowers and vulnerabilities that come with this. Together all these things will help you build a greater sense of self-awareness, making it easier for you to jump over those hurdles that have been holding you back for so long and start getting what you really want. It's time to dig deep and take a sledgehammer to those walls.

You will often hear people tell you that you are in charge of your own destiny, a statement that I couldn't agree with more. Which is why I can't express enough how important self-awareness is to goal achievement.

I wholeheartedly agree that you are in charge of your own life, but you will find that there are times where in order to get what you want, you will need to enlist the help of someone else. This tends to make hitting your goal a little more difficult. I mean, it's hard when the only person you have to work with is yourself, let alone someone else. What do you do when this happens? Well, sure you could just try to set goals that don't rely on the involvement of anyone else, but of course that's just not realistic. I want you to get what you want, not what is easiest.

What are the goals that might include someone else? Well, there are more than you might think. There is the big one of starting a family. It doesn't matter how much you try, if your goal is to marry the love of your life and have the 2.5 kids, then it's definitely going to take more than just you to make that happen. Then there are the smaller goals like getting a job promotion; sure it's up to you to put in the hard work and put your name forward. But the ultimate decision as to whether or not you get the job is up to someone else.

Just because someone else is required to reach your goals doesn't mean you should relinquish all control and abandon ship. It is still YOUR goal and even if someone else might have the deciding vote, it doesn't mean you don't have control or at least some form of influence.

The second part of this book focuses on the 'WE thing'. This is all about you learning to work with others to ultimately get what you want. After all, teamwork does make the dream work. I will teach you why it is easier for you to work with some more than others and how making small adaptations can help you to communicate, collaborate and cooperate more effectively. I will also teach you my six-step process for persuasion, a system that has been effective in my own life and that of my clients.

Before we go any further I want you to look back at the goals you just set yourself. Ask yourself is this a 'ME thing' or a 'WE thing'? In other words, can you do this completely by yourself or does it have the involvement of someone else somewhere?

Answer this question for each goal, and put them into the correlating column below. On the left, write any goals that fit into the 'ME thing', any 'WE things' place in the right column. This should take you two minutes.

Me Thing	We Thing

I expect that you have goals sitting on both sides of the table. If this isn't the case then don't think that means you can skip a part and take the fast track to the finish, we already know that doesn't work. Understanding how to deal with both a 'ME thing' and a 'WE thing' is important. I want to make it clear that just because you have assigned a goal to the 'WE thing' list, it doesn't mean you can ignore everything in the first part of the book. Even when your goal includes someone else, the outcome is still based on what you do; self-awareness is always going to be key to getting what YOU want.

CASE STUDY: MEET JO...

The Situation

Mum of two, Jo, set up her business, Dog First Aid, for two reasons. The first being a lover of all things furry with four legs and the second being she wanted a career that would fit around her children. Several years later and Jo has got her business off to a fantastic start but she is still struggling to achieve the work-life balance and financial freedom she had always set her sights on.

The Problem

Jo had worked with lots of different coaches over the years to develop her SMART goals and turn her dreams into reality, yet there was still something missing. She knew what she wanted and she had been doing all the right things: she set the goals, she made them SMART and developed a to-do list. But this never seemed to bring her closer to the finish post, she struggled to see the goals for anything more than just a list on her phone.

She couldn't figure out what was missing. She had worked with numerous coaches, taken all the advice she could get, she was doing everything she should be doing, but her progress felt stilted.

One of the big problems she had was that the achievement of her goals, especially those centred around her business and financial freedom, was dependent on others.

The Win-Win

Jo had always had an understanding of SMART goals and how they worked but what she was missing was how to bridge the gap from where she was to where she wanted to be. By working together, we figured out how we could break down her big goals and turn them into short- and mid-term goals, planning daily and weekly actions that could help bring her closer to achieving her big goals little by little.

Jo also learned how to distinguish the goals as either a 'ME thing' or a 'WE thing' and what this meant. Doing this helped her to become less frustrated as she could see that even when her goal success was dependent on others there was a lot she could do to impact the situation and move things forward.

"I had used all of the methods under the sun, but it always felt like something was missing. Understanding the 'ME thing' and 'WE thing' was like a lightbulb moment, for the first time it felt like all the jigsaw pieces came together."

The Techniques

Having SMART goals is a great place to start, you will struggle to move forward without them, but like Jo, if they are really big long-term goals you need to find a way to bridge the gap from where you are now to where you want to be in five years or so. The best way of doing this is to do what Jo did and break down the massive goals into smaller ones with daily actions that will create a steady momentum and keep you focused.

The second thing Jo was struggling with was how she felt out of control and stilted because her goals were heavily reliant on others. By dividing her goals into the two categories she could instantly see the things that she had direct control over, and the things that had shared control. Later on in the book I will expand on the actions and methods Jo used and explain how you can use them, in the same way, to impact goals even when they are considered to be a 'WE thing'. You are always in control of YOUR goal.

Busy Doin' Life

Usually when I ask someone what they think holds them back from getting what they want, one of the most common answers I get is time. Time eludes them. There are never enough hours in the day. Time just flies. They tell me that they are too busy just doin' life let alone trying to do all the other things they actually want to do. I understand this feeling, time is like a thief in the night and sometimes it doesn't matter how hard you try, you always feel like you're chasing your tail. We all experience this feeling at some point. I hate to break it to you but there have been and will always be only 24 hours in a day, that isn't going to change. You can't magic up hours, days or months, but you can change how you manage your time.

Before we get into the nitty-gritty, you first need to learn how to make time for achieving your goals. I am going to share with you my simple time management technique, I call it Alison Edgar's Big Balls. It is based on the Eisenhower Matrix (EISENHOWER, 2016), a method which you may also have seen Stephen Covey use in his rocks, pebbles and sand in a jar video.

The Eisenhower Matrix uses two factors to categorise tasks: important and urgent. This is a great technique to organise your daily life, it's also a really good tool to help you analyse how you distribute your time and whether or not you're dedicating it to the right things. But personally, I think it is confusing before you do something to think ooohh is this urgent and important or just important not urgent? If you don't understand something you will never implement and use it. Like I said, time is one of the biggest thieves to stop you getting what you want, so by adopting Alison Edgar's Big Balls will buy back time in your day to help you feel more in control and able to SMASH IT!

1. **Basketballs - Important and Urgent**

   There are tasks that are both important and urgent. Have you ever had a basketball to the face? Yep, that's how it feels when you forget about one of these tasks. They are important to you and time precious, therefore they are your priority and come before anything else. Drop the ball and it will take you a while to recover from this one.

2. **Tennis Balls - Urgent**

   These are things that might not necessarily be of the most importance but need to be done sooner rather than later. You'll think you can ignore them but they soon build up and before you know it you're trying to juggle 11 tennis balls like you're a clown act at the circus. Don't let them build up as this will only result in you feeling overwhelmed and overworked. If you're not careful these will become Basketballs.

3. **Ping-Pong Balls - Important**

   These are the things that are important to you but are not urgent. They will happily bounce around in the background while you focus on more urgent tasks. However, you do have to be careful not to fall into the trap of letting them bounce around forever, like tennis balls, they have an ability to multiply at rapid rates.

4. **Neither Important nor Urgent**

   This is the final category, these tasks do not get assigned a ball. If something is neither urgent nor important to you, then you should be questioning why it is even in your life. Anything that falls into this category can be crossed off or tossed into the trash immediately. They are not adding anything to your life and probably stopping you from getting what you want.

Now, when it comes to organising your day, week, month or even your year (I bet you thought I was about to break out into the *Friends* theme tune), most people use a linear to-do list. This doesn't allow us to prioritise the most important things, and we usually end up doing the things we enjoy or that take the least amount of time first, leaving the laborious tasks we don't like till the end. This means we can drop the ball or become overwhelmed, resulting in procrastination and sometimes getting nothing done!

It's a personal preference, but I like to use an online tool called Trello to manage my balls. You should have four lists: Basketballs, Tennis Balls, Ping-Pong Balls and Yay it's done! (you probably won't need this one if you're using paper as you can just score it off). The Trello app makes it easy for me to move the balls from one list to another; remember that does happen, what starts out as a Tennis Ball could very well end up a Basketball if you leave it too long.

For example, buying Granny's present for her birthday on 15th December might start as a Ping-Pong Ball in September; at the beginning of November it will have become a Tennis Ball, but if you ignore it, come December 14th it's going to be at the top of your Basketballs, about to hit you in the face at any moment, as well as being in Mum and Granny's bad books (we've all been there!).

I look at my three lists on Trello every day and plan what needs doing when based on how long I think the task will take, and which list it sits on. At the end of the day I review my lists, cross off the tasks I have completed, add anything for the next day and so on. Wherever you decide to write your lists and how often you decide to review them is up to you, but make sure you follow the system. If anything has been on the list too long, it's OK to dump it! Alison Edgar's Big Balls helps you to see what is important and what really isn't!

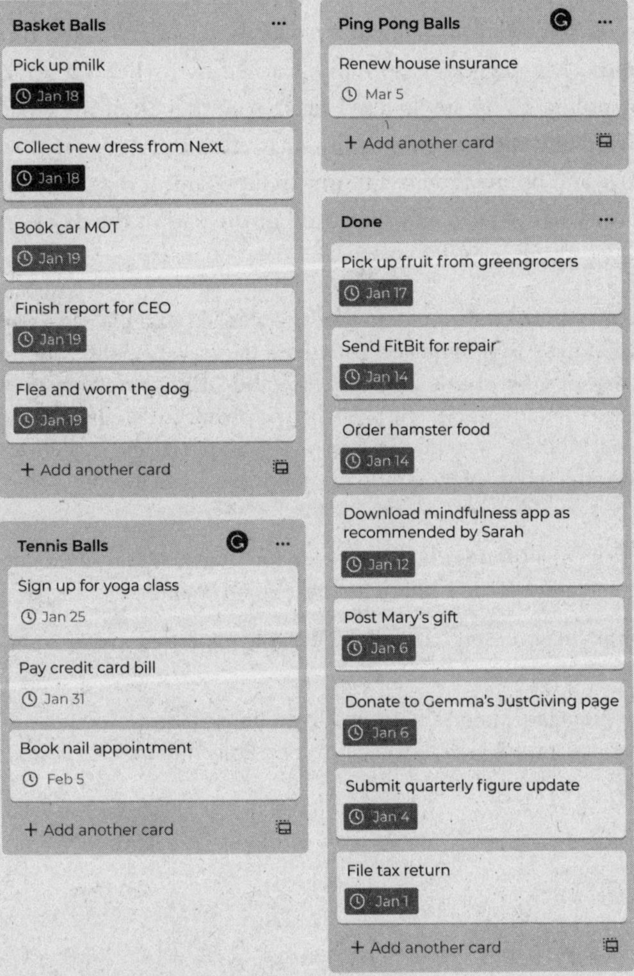

Other things which steal our time are emails and social media inhalation! Let's look at them individually and how we can also use Alison Edgar's Big Balls to take back control.

Notifications are one of my biggest pet peeves. They contribute massively to overwhelm, and this newfound social media world makes everything feel like it's urgent and needs to be done yesterday. Everybody feels entitled to your time, but the truth is when your inbox is stacked full of emails or DMs you don't have time for anybody. My biggest lesson I've learned is to live by an empty inbox policy. Every single day I make sure that all of my emails are answered and filed away, or if not answered, I've designated them a ball size and popped them into my Trello board. It massively reduces my overwhelm, and I can switch off at the end of the day knowing that everything is under control.

I want you to think about an average week in your life. On a piece of paper, or on your device, list all the things you spend your time doing on a daily basis. This should include everything from seeing friends, going to work and washing the dishes to scrolling through social media and going to the gym. Be as specific as you can. Now using the table below, plot these things based on their importance to you and level of urgency.

For anything important and urgent that needs completing immediately, place it under the Basketball column.

For anything urgent but not necessarily important, place it under the Tennis Ball column.

For anything important to you that doesn't necessarily have a deadline, place it under the Ping-Pong Ball column.

Basketballs	Tennis Balls	Ping Pong Balls

Looking at the table you just completed, do you think that you distribute your time effectively? How many things have you got on your list that you couldn't place as being important or urgent? It's too easy to get caught up not only in your day to day but pleasing other people and their dramas too, I'll come back to this later. We are often so busy doing life that we don't really have time to stop and think about our long-term goals and what we want our lives to look like.

CASE STUDY: MEET ROSE...

The Situation

Owner of Rose Hill Designs, Rose is an award-winning graphic artist balancing her love for art, animals, and being a parent. She has always been a keen list-maker, spending her days trying to maximise every minute so that she can do more of what she loves.

The Problem

As a self-managed artist and businesswoman, Rose felt like she was always chasing her tail. She has always been fond of writing to-do lists and loves the little buzz of satisfaction she gets every time she crosses something off. The problem was the list seemed to be getting longer and longer, yet the hours in the day felt like they were getting shorter and shorter.

When it came to her work life, Rose felt like she was the queen of organisation, she always knew what she was doing, when she was doing it and where she was supposed to be. The problem was her life outside of work; she never has enough time for her other biggest passion in life – her family and friends. She never missed a beat when it came to her business, but when it came to organising home life it felt like she couldn't catch a break.

Although she had always been a list-maker when it came to working, she still worked what felt like every hour of every day. There was always something else that needed to be done before she could switch off and start embracing her personal life. There was no balance.

The Win-Win

Rose learned about Alison Edgar's Big Balls time management system. This is when she realised that although she may have been making lists, actually they weren't always very well organised and didn't utilise her time.

Rose learned to organise her one linear list into three lists, prioritising tasks based on their level of importance and urgency. One of the things she found when doing this was that she had accumulated a lot of tasks on her list that actually were neither important nor urgent and were actually taking her time away from doing other things. The other thing she did was extend her lists to include home tasks and not just work ones; that way she could see the main Basketball in her life as a whole and was able to make a better judgment on where her time should be spent.

Rose said her time management skills were put to the ultimate test when organising her daughter's fourth birthday party. Anyone who has organised a child's birthday party will know that it's the equivalent of a royal extravaganza but with the added pressure of 20 excitable children. At the same time as wrapping presents, baking a cake, making party games, buying and preparing food, prizes, party bags and organising children and their parents, Rose also had a huge work project due, which only added to the pressure.

But with the balls in her court, Rose remained calm and in control. Not only did she get her project complete but the party was a hit. "My daughter, her friends and the parents all had the best time! Some of the mums even said I should go into hosting kids' parties. The Big Balls have been invaluable in helping to organise my time."

The Techniques

There are a lot of people who write lists and lists to organise their time yet still feel like they have none at the end of the day. In actual fact, they become a bit like Rose and the list almost becomes a distraction preventing them from doing what they really want. By organising her lists into Basketballs, Tennis Balls and Ping-Pong Balls, Rose could easily see what tasks should be done first, which ones should be done last and which ones were actually a complete waste of time. A lot of people include things on their lists that don't bring value to their lives but instead block them from achieving their goals.

One of the things that Rose did really well was applying the Big Balls to all aspects of her life to build a clear picture. By looking at both personal and work tasks, she was able to create a better balance between the two and do more of what she loves.

I will ask you again. What is stopping you from getting what you want? Is it really time or is it a lack of confidence, a fear of failure, or perhaps the fact you're not really sure if you want it at all? Maybe you're not the problem, maybe it's someone or something else. Perhaps they are blocking you, but then we do all have choices and we are in control of deciding whether or not we achieve our goals.

If you're spending all of your time scrolling through social media or procrastinating, then this is the kick up the ass you need. This is your reality check. The first thing you need to do is be honest with yourself and admit what is really stopping you from getting what you want. It's easy to look around at your life and blame time, or a lack of it, for not having what you want. When you use my Big Balls method, you'll soon see that time isn't the problem... YOU are!

THE
'ME THING'

WHY DO YOU WANT IT?

Now that you know what you want and you've made your goals SMART, you're ready to hit the ground running and put a plan into action. Well not quite. If you thought the hard part was done, I'm sorry because I'm about to throw you a bit of a curveball. If "What do you want?" was the six-million-dollar question, then "Why do you want it?" might seem damn near impossible. But don't worry, I'm here to help.

This section of the book is designed to make you think and question yourself. It's a bit like being on the popular TV quiz game show *Who Wants to be a Millionaire?* You've made it through the rounds, you've already made it further than ever before and you feel at the top of your game, all you have to do is answer this one last question and you get to take home the whopping cash prize. But try as you might, you just can't find the answer to this one, so you turn to your trusty game show host, in this case me, to use your lifelines and help you uncover the answer.

The reason this question stumps most people is that it's one they don't usually think about. To achieve your goal, you obviously need to know what it is you actually want as you found out in the previous section, but the real question you need to ask is why.

Why do YOU want it?

Looking back at your SMART goals, why do you want those things? Had you even thought about this when you were writing your list of goals?

Losing Sight of Why

'Big boned'! That was always my Mum's way of describing me. Never overweight or obese as is now the more common way to describe holding extra pounds. I grew up in Scotland where deep-fried food is a bit of a national obsession, from pizza (yes, deep fried pizza!) to haggis and Mars bars. A lot of our eating habits are formulated in our youth, and although my parents didn't have much spare money, any that they did have went on food-type treats. If I did something good, I would be rewarded with a sweet treat; if I had a bad day, "There, there, have some cake to commiserate." I'm sure you can relate to this – it was basically the norm for parenting at that time.

Over the years, my husband and I had jumped on the hamster wheel of life, juggling work and our boys the best we could. As our lives became fuller, time started to evaporate and convenience became the norm. We would fill our stomachs with whatever was quick and easy to grab, takeaways were more than a regular occurrence. I enjoyed nothing more than putting my feet up at the end of the day and indulging in a King Prawn Rezala from the local curry house with a big glass of white wine. As our collection of takeaway menus grew, so did our waistlines, the pounds kept piling on and on.

Every now and again, usually at New Year, I would take up a new fad diet and invest in a new 30-day gym pass to try and drop a few pounds, but it would never last. My motivation always dwindled, and I was quite happy with how I looked, sure I was a little overweight, I always would be, I was 'big boned'. Nevertheless, I thought I looked great.

However, 2005 was different, this was my most successful period at work ever. I have always been a top performer in every job I have done. I'm hard-working, skilled and focused but this period was outstanding, everything I touched turned to gold dust. A specific highlight was from one account who was spending £100 with my company. All my previous colleagues had just sent the paperwork in the post to the customer, but I decided to drive out to his farm in deepest, darkest Wiltshire to discover he was spending £10,000 with our biggest competitor; not for long, at the end of the visit his full spend went to me. This along with other similar accounts led to me being 3000% (yes, 3000%!) over target. It gave me a real kick in my step, because not only would I see the benefit in my wage packet but I would also be odds-on favourite to win a place at the international achiever's event.

I started to visualise myself on the podium collecting my award in front of all my peers and senior managers, but wait... what was I going to wear? I was 'big boned' and most of the females who joined the company I worked for had a certain 'top end' image and look. I had never been overly concerned with my image before this point, but for some reason, this time I wanted to look like them. I knew that the moment I stepped on stage to collect my award, I would be compared to previous winners. I wanted to adorn the stage with my super skinny dress like the other winners I had seen the years before!

My vanity to be thin was starting to rule my thoughts.

I started a new diet and fitness regime, this time I was determined to see results. My new plan meant I was eating healthier and exercising more. But I didn't want to be healthy, I wanted to be thin so people would compliment me on my looks. My WHY was vanity, not health.

All was going swimmingly and weight was starting to fall off, my body was shrinking and the thought of wearing small-size clothes was within my reach. I was the same size then as I was in my teens, even after having my two babies. My energy levels were so high I wanted to keep exercising and pushing faster and faster. Wow, I was going to look AMAZING collecting the award on stage!!

I would attend work meetings with my colleagues and have streams of people telling me how well I looked, and the weight loss really suited me. I was loving the attention for my new-found shape. It was at one of these meetings my boss at the time asked me why my hand was shaking. Shaking, I hadn't really noticed, but there it was. When I held my hand out with a glass of water it was like there was an earthquake and water was sloshing around the glass. He marched me out of the meeting to the doctor's surgery straight away, where I waited for the blood test.

Now, we all know blood tests can take weeks to come back, but at 9am the next morning I was asked to come to the surgery to start medication. They had diagnosed an overactive thyroid, and the reason for the weight loss was not from my hard work at the gym, but my immune system was fighting against itself and it was causing my heart to pump at a dangerous rate.

Beta blockers were prescribed to stabilise my heart rate and carbimazole to counteract the thyroid levels, but a couple of weeks later I noticed something strange going on with my eyesight. Two things were happening: one it felt like I had conjunctivitis and the other was I could not look up, down or side to side without using my head, my eyeballs were failing to function.

I was diagnosed with thyroid eye disease and superior limbic keratitis which then led to a concoction of drugs with strong side effects, which still ultimately were not improving my eyesight. But on a really positive note, I was still not gaining weight, so I would still look great at the awards ceremony!

I can vividly remember the day the consultant told me that drastic action was required. The appointments were running late, and I had been in the waiting room with both my children for what felt like an eternity. Realistically it was probably only an hour or so, but I'm sure any parent reading will know this is a stressful environment for anyone, trying to keep two kids occupied, not squabbling or annoying the other patients. It's no mean feat.

It felt like the world stopped around me when the consultant told me the only way to save my sight was to undergo an intensive course of radiotherapy on my eyes. But please don't judge me when I say this, the shock wasn't because of the treatment, it was when they told me that I would have to start a course of strong steroids. Nooooo… all the weight I had lost would be going back on… the dress, the award!!

When I re-evaluated the situation and put things into perspective, of course I realised how absurd it was that losing my sight and never being able to see my children was not my priority. I had got so caught up in the idea of looking thin that my initial reaction was completely irrational.

I'm glad to say that after the radiotherapy my sight was returned to its former glory; as for the awards… well I guess it wasn't my year because I didn't win. However, the commission I earned that period did provide a family trip with Neil and the boys to Disneyland Paris in the Magic Castle, creating long-lasting family memories, which let's face it is far more valuable than any award or size 10 dress.

One of the main reasons people fail to hit their goal is because they don't know why they want it in the first place. If your why isn't strong enough you will find it's easy to lose track of your goal and let it pass by the wayside. As soon as you hit a bump in the road, you'll be ready to dump your goal quicker than the *Love Island* contestants at a recoupling. Whereas when you know why you want something and that why is really strong, it helps to keep your mind focused on the end result. There are no right or wrong answers to this question, only you will know why you want something and whether or not it really matters to you deep, deep down.

I could have continued to lose weight after the radiotherapy if I had really wanted, but I didn't, because my why wasn't strong enough. I didn't want it for the right reasons and when it comes down to it the need for vanity is short-lived and will never suppress the cravings for a deep-fried Mars bar. Fast forward several years and I have lost three stone and managed to keep it off for well over two years, I regularly exercise either attending circuit class with Neil or running on my own. And as you already know, I have even hit my goal of running a half marathon. If someone had told me two years ago that I would be a regular at ParkRun on Saturday mornings, I would have laughed in their face.

So, what has changed? My WHY has. When I tried to lose weight before it was always for vanity reasons, it was never because I was unhappy but more because I feared people judging me. I was trying to lose weight for everyone else, not myself. My WHY wasn't strong. Now I choose to eat healthily and exercise for health reasons. A couple of years ago I was running around London from place to place as I normally would, I was climbing up the escalators in the tube station, rushing to get to a meeting. When I got to the top I had to physically stop and get my breath back.

This wasn't the first time I had noticed my lack of fitness, there had been multiple times over the past year where I had come home from a meeting or long day at work and realised I was absolutely knackered. I know it's normal to get tired, but I was physically exhausted, my weekends had become about recouping and getting ready to face another week. I didn't have the energy to enjoy family time or take Hovis – my Cocker Spaniel and third son – out for long walks in our lovely countryside.

As I stood there at the top of that escalator with the world rushing past me, everything hit me. I had two parents who passed away from a stroke and didn't get to see their grandchildren grow up. I didn't want the same for me. I want to watch my two sons graduate from university, I want to watch them grow up and get married and have children of their own. I want to be there to play with my future grandchildren. How was I going to manage any of that if I could barely manage to climb the stairs?

This reality check was exactly what I needed. It made me realise that I wasn't healthy and that I needed to make a lifestyle change. My WHY to keep fit is stronger now than it has ever been, I don't care what others think of me, I never have but I do care about my family and being able to make the most of every moment with them. When I think about this it becomes easy to pick up my trainers and go running, even on the mucky rainy days when I would rather do anything else.

Something I always say is when your why is strong it's hard to go wrong!

Revisit your goals and jot down in the box the reason WHY you want them. You may find that your goals aren't actually what you want if the WHY isn't strong enough. Take any goals off your vision board that are deviating from your ultimate direction, goals without a strong WHY will deflate you and cause you to not achieve anything at all. This may take a few minutes to think through.

WHY DO YOU WANT IT?

Maslow's Hierarchy 101

During the research for this book, I decided to look into goals and where they come from. What makes us want these things? This is when I came across Maslow's Hierarchy of Needs and realised how this theory underpinned our everyday lives and how integral it is to goal setting. It was grasping this concept that made me feel I had finally understood the meaning of life.

I had heard of Maslow's Hierarchy of Needs before, but I had never really understood it or its significance until I started my research. The more I read about it, the more it completely revolutionised my way of thinking.

Before I begin, I want to clarify that I am not a psychologist, I am sharing my views and interpretations based on what I have found to be helpful in my own personal life and that of my clients.

Now you may already be well acquainted with Maslow's work but just in case you're not I will give you a brief introduction. In 1943 Abraham Maslow wrote and published a paper called 'A Theory of Human Motivation' in which he aimed to define what motivates our behaviour. To put it simply, he set out to discover why we do what we do. Maslow developed a five-tier model, often referred to as the Hierarchy of Needs.

Maslow (1943, 1954) said that people are motivated to achieve specific needs and some needs will take precedence over others. Maslow's original hierarchy defines human needs into five categories: physiological, safety, belonging and love, esteem and self-actualisation. The model is displayed in a pyramid structure (see image below) and like a traditional hierarchy, you have to work your way up from the bottom to top.

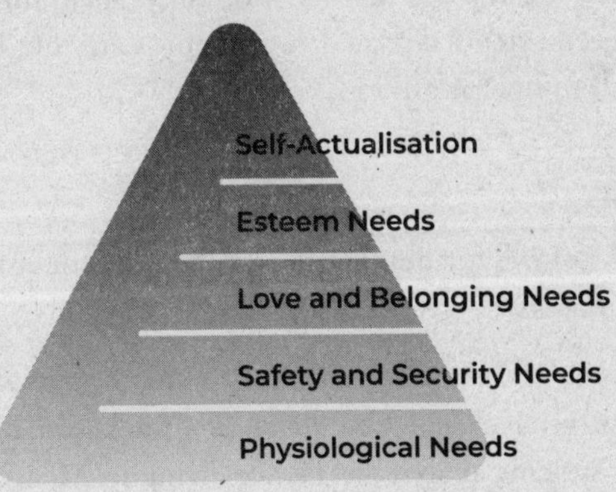

As humans, our most basic need is for physical survival, hence why physiological needs are at the bottom of the pyramid. Once we have fulfilled the needs at that level, we are then motivated to achieve the needs in the next level and so on until we reach the top of the pyramid. It's a little bit like a video game: every time you complete a round you get to level up with each level becoming increasingly difficult, and if you fail the level you drop back down to the tiers below and have to complete it again.

Everyone has the potential to reach the top of Maslow's Hierarchy of Needs; however, progress is often disturbed by life experiences – birth, death, marriage and divorce are all examples of this (McLeod, 2018). Sometimes it is affected by things outside of our control too, like the COVID-19 pandemic. This explains why we are motivated by different things at different points in our lives and also how a big life event can completely change things for us.

There have been many adjustments and additions to Maslow's Hierarchy of Needs since it was first established and it has been expanded to include three extra layers: cognitive, aesthetic and transcendent. I will keep things simple by focusing on the original five-tier model, but I thought it was worth mentioning how the model has been extended should you want to carry out some of your own research to find out more.

Cast Away

To explain Maslow's further, I want to tell you a little story about my friend Tom Hanks.

In 1995, Tom, not actually a friend of mine (I only wish), starred in the hit survival drama *Cast Away* as Chuck Noland. Chuck is a successful systems analyst for FedEx, living in Memphis with his long-term beloved girlfriend Kelly. At this point, you could say his character is sitting pretty, somewhere between the top two tiers. His basic physiological needs are being met, he is both physically and financially secure and has the love of a good woman. Based on what we know about his job, I think it's fair to say he's well accomplished and respected in his field which helps fulfil his esteem needs. I would say on Maslow's he is probably hovering around the fourth and fifth tiers, trying to make the move from esteem to self-actualisation.

Things are looking pretty good for Tom until he has to fly to Malaysia on an emergency business trip. During his flight there is a huge storm, causing the plane to crash land in the middle of the ocean. Very unexpected and something that was out of his control, a little bit like the COVID-19 pandemic. Tom manages to escape the sinking plane and soon realises he is the only one that survived the crash. He later drifts to shore, where he finds himself alone on a deserted island with nothing but the FedEx packages that got washed up with him.

His initial reaction is to try and leave the island in the hopes of getting rescued. He inflates a life raft and begins to paddle out to sea, but as he gets closer to the end of the reef the waves start crashing in. The sea overpowers him, he is tossed out of his life raft and pinned underwater by the waves injuring himself on the harsh coral. He gets washed back to shore not only with a deflated life raft but a deflated sense of hope.

Just like that, our buddy Tom has fallen from the top of the hierarchy to the very bottom. He's gone back to basics, with his only goal to survive until he gets found. This is where natural human instincts come into play, putting our physiological needs before anything else. Tom knows that if he is going to survive, he will need to find water, food and shelter, the basic biological requirements all humans need to live.

While searching the island for food and water, Tom starts opening the FedEx packages to see if they contain anything that will help aid his survival. He chooses to open all the packages except one. He makes a promise to deliver that one last package. This is the physical embodiment of his WHY. On the days when he is fed up, lonely and feels like he can't possibly make it through another day on the island, he can see the package and remembers the promise he made to deliver it. The package represents his goal to survive and make it home.

As the film continues, we see Tom move up the hierarchy; even on the small island where there is little hope, the hierarchy of needs and desire to move towards the top still exists. It's human nature to want to progress. Tom gets to a point where he can satisfy the majority of his physiological needs. He has learned how to spearfish, he knows how to start fires to keep warm, and has fashioned himself some basic form of clothing. He makes a cave home, providing him with somewhere secure to settle and he no longer fears the island, he fulfils his security and safety needs.

When it comes to belongingness and love, poor Tom has no one. This is when he comes across Wilson, a volleyball with a face of sorts. OK, so maybe it's not the conventional two-way relationship that springs to mind when you think of love and belonging, but it works for Tom. Wilson becomes his confidant, and we see him talking and arguing with Wilson on a regular basis. Having Wilson comforts him and satisfies his need for company. Although it may be unconventional, Tom develops a friendship with Wilson and can rely on him to get through the tough days when he feels alone. Luckily, today we have brilliant technology, and since we aren't stranded on a desert island, most of us have been able to keep in touch with our families during the pandemic, which has been a great coping mechanism.

Slowly but surely, Tom is creeping his way back up the tiers. Sure, things are a little different this time around, but so are his surroundings. You could even say that he begins to fulfil his esteem needs as he is no longer just surviving but he is starting to thrive confidently, knowing that he has done everything he possibly can to keep himself alive.

It's when he realises that no one is going to rescue him that he starts working on a plan to build a raft and leave the island. I'm going to go out on a limb here and say that we could argue Tom is at the very same tipping point he was at before the plane crash. He's back at that line between esteem and self-actualisation. All his deficiency needs have been met, he knows he is meant for more, and if he is ever going to achieve his goal of delivering that one last package then he will have to take action and make it happen because no one is going to do it for him. His attempt to get rescued and leave the island is his way of striving for self-actualisation.

Apologies if you haven't seen the film, I guess this was a bit of a spoiler (but you have had since 1995 to watch it!). I think it is a great example, albeit quite an extreme one, of how Maslow's theory works and impacts our lives. It shows that the hierarchy exists within us all, no matter our environment or surroundings. I think it also shows us that despite the pandemic, or any other setbacks that the universe throws our way, there are coping mechanisms we can implement to get ourselves back up the hierarchy.

Tom always wanted to get off the island but before he could do that he needed to learn how to survive. Just to spoil it completely, Tom does get rescued after floating out at sea on his raft and eventually gets to return home. He didn't make it the first time he tried because he wasn't ready; even if he had made it past the reef, he would never have survived because you can't achieve something that is high up on your hierarchy when you're stuck at the bottom. He needed to learn how to look after himself and figure out a plan before he could paddle out into the middle of the ocean and get rescued.

Now that I've given you a bit of an introduction to Maslow and his Hierarchy of Needs, I am going to break down each level further to help you understand your own behaviour a little bit more and hopefully also bring you closer to discovering your WHY.

Back to Basics

The first tier of Maslow's Hierarchy of Needs are the basic biological requirements needed for human survival. These are air, food, shelter, clothing, warmth, sex and sleep. Maslow considered physiological needs to be more important than any of the other needs in the hierarchy, as the human body needs these things in order to function at its optimal level.

The physiological needs are the most important because we literally cannot survive without them. They may be at the bottom of the hierarchy, but we put them above all else. Your basic needs are the only group in Maslow's that you will come across every day of your life. It does not matter whether you are a fancy hotshot lawyer or stay at home parent, every day you will dedicate some of your time to fulfilling your physiological needs. To fulfil these basic needs is the one goal we all share as humans. The motivation behind fulfilling these basic goals is so strong because we know what will happen if we don't: we won't survive.

Safety First

The second rung on the ladder of Maslow's hierarchy is safety needs. These are still considered to be part of our basic needs but start to become more complex than our physiological ones. At this level, the desire to feel safe and secure becomes our primary focus. This includes our health and wellness, financial security, job stability and protection against injury, harm and feelings of fear. It is at this stage that people are often trying to establish some kind of control and order into their lives.

Like Tom Hanks in *Cast Away*, we all have an innate drive to survive. It goes back to the caveman era and Darwin's Evolutionary theory of survival of the fittest. Subconsciously and sometimes consciously we know that reduced risks mean increased safety and ultimately a better chance of survival. Therefore, safety and security are considered basic human needs.

How does this relate to goal setting? The purpose of this whole section is to help you identify why you desire certain things in life and why some of these desires are more important to you than others, or at least they should be. It makes sense that finding a steady job and moving to an area with a low crime rate would be more important to you than buying a new car. It's not going to matter that you can drive around in your flash new whip if you don't have a house to live in or you fear for your life every time you have to get in your car and drive to the shops.

One of the things I find most interesting about this level of Maslow's hierarchy is that it is also why a lot of people do not progress. According to Maslow, it is difficult to fulfil needs further up on the hierarchy when you have not fulfilled the basics. But when it comes to safety and security, I think even when we have it, we struggle to move up a level or achieve self-actualisation, as this sometimes means risking what we have already achieved. It's not the lack of safety and security that is the blocker for some people but the fear of losing the safety and security they already have.

The Power of Love

When we reach rung three on Maslow's ladder, we start to move from basic physiological needs to more social and emotional needs, which takes us from surviving to thriving. As humans, we crave a sense of belonging and being part of a pack. Some people prefer large groups, others smaller more intimate encounters. This can include friends, clubs, gangs, teams, online communities, professional organisations or work colleagues. It comes back to our tribal instincts; we all yearn to be part of something.

This explains why so many people have struggled during the COVID-19 pandemic. They have had their relationships stripped from them and been thrown into isolation through no fault of their own. When I first explored Maslow's, I felt I had discovered the meaning of life and that all of my questions about why we feel the way we do had been answered. It's helped me to navigate the pandemic. Understanding that the loneliness you feel is just a part of Maslow's will help you to rationalise and build a coping strategy.

Dating is as old as Adam and Eve, but with the evolution of technology and apps like Tinder and Grindr being commonplace in today's society, it would be easy to believe that this rung is about a significant other half. Whilst it is important for some people to find the love of their life, it is also important to find a community to be part of. However, some people are so busy searching for 'the one' that they are blind to the support of their family and friends who are there no matter what their relationship status is on Facebook.

We have all had friends who drop us like a hot potato as soon as a new boyfriend or girlfriend comes on the scene, then comes running back with their hankie in hand when they get dumped, only to do it again with each time they swipe to the right and get a match. When it comes to love and belonging, it can be easy to get caught up in ideals of romantic love and forget about the feelings of belonging and fulfilment that come from being part of a family, friendship group or community.

We can see this the other way round when people become complacent within their relationships. You will often see when things are no longer new and exciting that individuals often crave to become part of something else. Sure, they feel loved by their partner and families, but they are missing the sense of belonging that comes with a nonromantic social group. It's at this point they might take up Zumba classes or join the local book club, in order to fulfil this need to belong and become accepted by a wider community.

Whilst a large part of successfully fulfilling these needs comes from intimate relationships and friendships, I do believe that there is an element of self-love that needs to be achieved. As the old adage goes, you have to learn to love yourself before anyone else can. I think this explains why some people, even when married with a family, cannot move past this rung on Maslow's ladder, whilst those who lack intimate relationships can. This explains why a single person who has a strong sense of self-love and a satisfying friendship group can achieve self-actualisation without having a romantic relationship.

I married my husband Neil in 1997. According to the Office of National Statistics (2019), 38% of the 272,536 marriages in that year have now ended in divorce. That doesn't include relationships of those who didn't quite make it to the altar. For some people, the loss of love and belonging when they go through a break-up sends them into a tailspin and they can't comprehend the emotions that they are feeling. As explained by Elizabeth Kubler-Ross (2014) in her 1969 research, when we lose somebody or something, be it through a break-up, a divorce or bereavement, we go through the five stages of grief.

STAGE 1: Denial

In this first stage, you try to pretend that nothing has changed, you deny the situation or think it's a mistake, attempting to continue life as normal. This is the brain's way of reducing overwhelm to protect you. It's like it's playing a trick on you, making you think you can continue as though nothing has changed, but soon you'll trip up.

For example, you forget that you can no longer pick up the phone to that person and have a chat, yet you don't remember this until the phone is in your hand and you're dialling the number. By this time, it's too late, the person has gone and it hits you like a ton of bricks, making you feel more alone than ever before.

STAGE 2: Anger

When experiencing a loss, you will be at the centre of a whirlwind of emotions. At this point it can be hard to express how you're feeling, anger seems like the only option. It seems easier to be angry at everything and everyone rather than admit how you're really feeling. You are even angry at yourself. Although this does help to express bottled-up emotions, you will usually separate yourself even further from those who are trying to support you. We take our anger out on the people closest to us, which only makes it harder for them to help, pushing all ideals of love and belonging further away.

STAGE 3: Bargaining

When you realise you can't change or influence the situation, you start to look for ways you can regain some form of control. Another part of this stage is what I call the 'what if?' when you try to revisit things that have happened in the past to get a different outcome. 'What if I was thinner?' or 'What if I had paid more attention to them?' Ultimately this is just a form of self-sabotage as nothing can change the results, all it does is make you second guess yourself, eating you up and leaving you frustrated. There is no winning in this situation, you cannot change the past or question whether another decision would have led to a different outcome because you will never truly know.

STAGE 4: Depression

This is when reality hits and the emotional fog begins to clear. You realise that no amount of denial, anger or bargaining can change what has happened and see the situation for what it really is. You feel utterly helpless, you've hit rock bottom, you feel your whole world has been taken from under your feet. It's at this point when you are usually knocked for six and start to retreat within yourself, even getting out of bed to meet your basic needs becomes an uphill struggle. Without addressing it, this stage can last for a long time. It's important to note that even if you are aware of the grieving process, you can't avoid this stage. Even if you push it back, it will likely rear its ugly head at some point in the future.

STAGE 5: Acceptance

This is the final stage, it's important to recognise that you still feel the pain of loss. Acceptance doesn't mean happiness, it means you have come to terms that you cannot get back the person you have lost, and you must now learn to carve a new path without them. This is when you start to regain sight of your WHY and recognise that love and belonging is still an option, it is still achievable. You begin to realise that you are the one in control of your own life and have a choice in what it looks like.

When we lose a loved one from our life for whatever reason, it can be life changing and things that once seemed important might no longer feel that way. Sometimes it's like pushing the reset button. These five stages of grief are the same when you go through any form of loss, whether it be a person, a pet, or even a job. When going through the stages it's a bit of a chicken and egg situation. You need to reach acceptance to find your WHY but you also need your WHY to drive you towards acceptance. There is no timestamp for these five stages and everyone goes through them at their own pace. The important thing is to know what stage you're at. When you know where you are it becomes easier to get where you are going.

This book is being written during the COVID-19 pandemic. Other than the loss of employment and financial instability which threatened our safety and security, one of the most difficult challenges almost every single person who has experienced lockdown has faced is not being able to meet with their close family and friends. For a lot of us, government regulations stated that we were not able to socialise with anyone outside of our household in person. This meant no Friday night drinks in the local, no hugging your mates, no visiting your brother, sister, mother or lover that does not live with you. For many, this has been one of the hardest things to endure.

Coming out of this, one of the biggest lessons that the world has learned is the importance of friends and family. Love and belonging is something we often take for granted, but the COVID-19 pandemic ensured everyone found a new respect for their community and external support systems. So much so that virtual chats, online quiz nights and video apps became a saving grace for those who felt isolated and alone, bringing to the forefront that for many, even in a materialistic society, nothing is more valuable than the power of love.

Esteem

The penultimate level of Maslow's hierarchy is self-esteem. There is some criticism of his theory. One of the reasons for this is that the theory is outdated; it was originally published in 1943, but life isn't the same as it was back then. In the '40s life was very linear. Most people were married by their early 20s, had children, settled down and stayed that way until they died. In the 21st century, life is more complex. People are no longer on the same linear path. The world is full of options and choices, which is why I think the levels of the hierarchy are still present motivators in our lives but don't necessarily fall in the same order for everyone. Even Maslow in the late 1980s pointed out that his theory isn't as rigid as he first thought.

In my opinion, the bottom two layers of the pyramid – the basic needs – haven't changed, we still need water, air, food and shelter to survive. Where it becomes more complex is when we reach the physiological needs: love and belonging and esteem. I think there is a lot of overlap between these two levels and the way in which someone goes through them will depend on each individual's personal circumstances.

So, what is esteem? The dictionary quite simply defines it as 'respect and admiration'. However, according to Maslow, esteem can be divided into two categories: low and high. He defines low self-esteem as the desire for respect from others, it is the reason we aim to achieve a certain status or build a reputation. High self-esteem on the other hand comes from within and is dependent on a number of factors such as; our achievements, behaviours, beliefs and personal perception of ourselves and others. I don't disagree with Maslow, however I think it's not as clear cut as being either high or low, I think esteem is a scale.

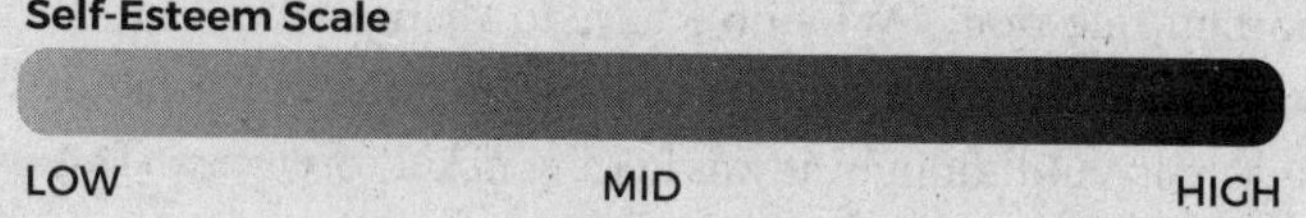

- Low - You don't ask for other people's opinion because you know you won't change your mind on how you see yourself. No matter what somebody else tells you, all you can see are the bad points, and if they do say something positive, you think they're only saying that to make you feel better.
- Mid - You regularly ask for other people's opinion and feedback in all aspects of your life, eg: "Do you think I look ok in this jacket?" or "Can you check this piece of work in case I've done it wrong?" Whilst you are learning to be

confident in yourself, you need the reassurance to boost your self-esteem.

- High - You are self-assured and unaffected by the feedback from others, whether it be positive or negative.

Someone with low self-esteem uses the words 'I don't care' as a defence mechanism when they receive negative feedback when in actuality they are cut to the core. Partly because they don't want others to see how easily they are impacted by third-party opinions as it indicates having low self-esteem, which they see as a weakness. I want you to know that it doesn't have to be a weakness. If you identify at the lower end of the scale that is OK! Knowing where you are is a great starting point.

While writing this section of the book I was asked to participate in a discussion on BBC Radio 5 Live with Nihal Arthanayake. The focus was on an article written by a young journalist, Grace Pritchard (2020), around The Myth of Meritocracy, who asked the very important question, "Why do I have to change who I am if I want to succeed?" Grace, a Yorkshire lass, was the first in her family to go to university and thought it was her big ticket to success. This wasn't the case. Instead, she found university to be a breeding ground for classism, her working-class background didn't fit in with the middle-class world of academia. She felt like she had to change who she was, and was even told by one of her tutors that she would achieve more success should she drop her thick Yorkshire accent.

Grace says, "In order to be what society deems as successful as a working-class person, you have to up and leave your home and abandon that part of you." This is why people get stuck at the wrong end of the scale, chasing the wrong dream and never really getting what they want. It goes back to what I said at the beginning, cut the wishy-washy language from your life. Learn to take those words and define them by your own standards. If you are forever chasing someone else's ideal of 'success' you will never get there, because you will always be waiting for their validation, waiting for them to tell you that you've achieved. That is low self-esteem, trying to earn someone else's respect by achieving their idea of success. It doesn't work.

"Why do I have to change who I am if I want to succeed?" My answer to this question is you don't. Changing who you are won't make you a success. It won't make you happy or free. You don't need to change who you are, you need to accept it. That's the secret.

You fear failure and rejection, that's why you don't get what you want. You do things because you think it will make other people love and accept you, when really what you should be doing is trying to love and accept yourself. To move from low to high self-esteem, you need to accept who you are, and to do that you need to know who you are. But why is having high self-esteem so important to getting what YOU want? To put it simply, if you don't believe in yourself, nobody else will believe in you either.

Where do you think you sit on the self-esteem scale? Draw an arrow on the scale below as to where you think you currently sit. Be honest with yourself.

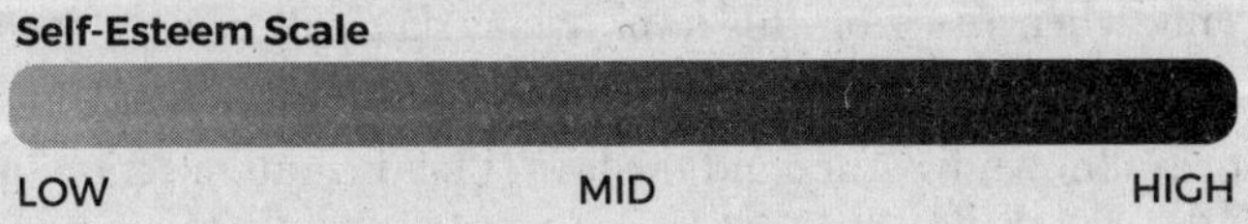

How can you learn to love yourself? How do you accept yourself? How do you become self-aware? I'm sure that's what you really want to know. Unfortunately, there is no one simple answer to that question, if that was the case you probably wouldn't be reading this book. Like I said, high self-esteem develops as a result of a number of factors. The rest of the 'ME thing' section is dedicated to helping you gain self-awareness and understanding yourself; I truly believe that when you do this, getting what you want will become a lot easier. There are four things that I believe will help you become more self-aware:

1. Understanding your motivation - This is what we are working on now as we work through Maslow's hierarchy.
2. Knowing your mindset - Identifying your mindset, how to change it and understanding the important role it plays.
3. Understanding your behaviour - Knowing why you act and react in the way that you do and how this holds you back and spurs you on.
4. Recognising you have both superpowers and vulnerabilities and being OK with it.

Like with any of the levels on Maslow's hierarchy, just because you have achieved it once it doesn't mean you will have it forever. Self-esteem is exactly the same. It's hard to move up the scale but when you reach a high level of self-esteem it does help to stabilise you a little. However, life does happen and things do change and you might find yourself moving back and forth. This is why self-actualisation is rare, it's difficult to maintain a consistently high level of self-esteem. Especially when reaching this level means you will usually want to challenge yourself and push to strive for new things. When you dive into the unknown it's scary and the fear of failure and rejection often comes flooding back, which ultimately pushes you back towards low self-esteem.

I want to tell you about my spare room (a bit weird, I know). In my old house, I always had a pristine spare room, ready and waiting for guests at any point. I always thought that was the expectation. We lived in a four-bedroom house, Neil and I had a room, both the boys had their own room but they were tiny, and the fourth room was the immaculate guest room. The thing is we hardly ever had any guests. The boys were driving us up the wall with nowhere to play whilst a perfectly good room sat empty, just in case someone came to stay. We were struggling to live in a house 24/7 so that someone could come to stay with us four days a year and think the house was perfect. After a while, I realised how ridiculous this was and turned the guest room into a playroom for the boys.

An important thing to remember is you have to spend 24 hours a day, seven days a week with yourself for your whole life. It's great when someone tells you you've done a good job or thinks you're pretty or funny, but it doesn't mean anything if you don't believe those things yourself. Don't become someone you're not to please someone you see for 40 hours a week – it's like modelling your house around a guest who never visits. Be who you are and accept it for the person you have to spend every single day of your life with – yourself.

Hopefully, you can see how your level of esteem has a massive impact on getting what you want. When your esteem is low, your goals are often misguided and you spend more time trying to get what other people want rather than what you want. When you do finally figure out what you really want to achieve, you are too scared to go for it. This is one of the biggest obstacles for almost everyone, they don't believe in themselves. You need to know and accept who you are if you want to SMASH IT!

Tap O' The Hill

Self-actualisation is the final stage of Maslow's, the peak of the triangle, the top of the hill, or tap o' the hill as we say in Scotland! Reaching this stage doesn't promise eternal happiness, it is a need like any other level of the hierarchy and therefore requires fulfilment. The difference between this stage and the others is that fulfilment doesn't mean moving on up to another level, as there is nowhere to go. Self-actualisation is when the individual recognises life as a continual process of development and growth, seeking peak experiences and embracing the world for everything it can be. They enjoy the feelings of euphoria and joy that come with knowing this.

Everyone's version of the tap o' the hill is different. Self-actualisation is understanding that life isn't static, happiness isn't a destination, it's an ongoing process. Someone who is sitting on this level seeks to be the best they can, this can mean anything from being the best parent to becoming a world-renowned artist. It's about the individual person being the best possible version of themselves.

This can be hard to quantify. Like everything, I created a simplified solution to make it easy to understand self-actualisation and what it takes to get there. I've named the system The Banks of Balance, it's easy to follow. I divide my life into three key areas, or banks as I call them. It's depositing in each bank equally that helps achieve self-actualisation which in my opinion leads to happiness. Let's take a look at the banks:

Bank of Cash

This is important but it doesn't mean you have to be a billionaire; it just means you have to cover the bottom two levels of Maslow's hierarchy. When they set their goals, lots of people may have initially said 'rich'. But like any of those other wishy-washy words, what does this mean? I think when people say they want to be rich, what they really mean is they want the choices that come with lots of money. You don't need money to have a choice, you need clarity.

This bank is about being financially stable, whatever that means for you. Financial stability is important, it's like an oxygen mask, it's hard to achieve anything else when you can't breathe. However, it won't necessarily bring you happiness and freedom. Things that I put in my bank of cash are any work-related activities, really anything that generates money. Some people spend far too much time focusing on the bank of cash, leading to a lack of work-life balance. This leaves them vulnerable to slip back down to the lower levels of the hierarchy.

Bank of Give Back

Being the best version of you means something different for everyone. Your banks might look a little different from mine, but for me to be the best I can be means having a positive impact on the world and those in it. I think a lot of people also feel this way. Giving back feeds the soul, when you do good, you feel good. Some people donate money, I donate my time. I mentor startup entrepreneurs, help troubled teens and create employment for school and university leavers. My payback is watching them grow their confidence, spreading their wings and admiring from afar while they create their own pathway up the mountain of Maslow's.

But I would not be able to do that if my other banks weren't full, that's why balance is key. Giving back doesn't necessarily have to be to a cause or for somebody else. You can also give back to yourself. When you spend time exercising, studying or any other activities that you don't necessarily enjoy but can enhance your future, be it long-term or short, you are giving back to yourself.

Bank of Faffing Around

This is my favourite bank because, of course, it's my most enjoyable. For some people, 'Faffing Around' may have certain negative connotations. For example, when you're waiting in the car with the engine running and your partner is busy watering the plants and triple checking all of the windows are locked before you can possibly nip down to the supermarket, you may assume they are 'Faffing Around'. But for me, this bank is about spending time doing things you love. 'Faffing Around' for me is about doing the things that make your heart sing.

It can be anything from catching up on your favourite Netflix series, having a day out with your nearest and dearest, or spending time on your favourite hobby. Everyone wants to have fun; I am sure that at least one of your goals is set around something you love and enjoy. The secret, like any of the banks, is to keep it balanced. If you spend too much time faffing around, you'll lose sight of the bank of cash, which will also affect your level on the hierarchy.

Some of your goals may fit into more than one bank; for example, if I volunteer my time to help with an event for disadvantaged students, that feeds both my bank of faffing around and bank of giveback. I don't get paid, but I get to rock the stage, and I get to see the lightbulb moments from the young people when they gain new skills to enhance their lives.

According to Maslow, very few people make it to this self-actualisation, not because they're not capable, in theory we all have the ability to reach the top of the triangle. The problem sits further down the pyramid. As I have stated, the levels in Maslow's hierarchy do not necessarily fall in a specific order. However, one thing that doesn't change is that self-actualisation is always at the top and that the other levels need to be fulfilled to a certain degree, no matter their order, for someone to achieve it.

When my banks are balanced, I feel on top of the world, perhaps even Queen O' The Hill. Like any bank, mine need deposits to keep them full. When they are out of kilter so am I. I have viewed my life this way for many years, but now I realise that my banks aren't so different from Maslow's hierarchy. Compartmentalising my life this way has always helped me maintain a balance. It tells me what I need to do and where I need to make a deposit in order to reach the top of the mountain.

The problem is everyone wants to make it to the top of the hierarchy, even when they don't know it exists. However, they don't know why, and they don't know what it means. That's why you set the SMART goals at the beginning of the book, to give you direction. When someone doesn't know what they want, one of the default answers is always cash, they think winning the lottery will solve all their problems. I haven't won the lottery, but I can tell you it isn't the answer. Sure, it might make some things easier, secure those basic needs, but it can't buy you love and it definitely doesn't magically give you high self-esteem. This isn't Disneyland, you can't buy a fast-track pass to the top of the hierarchy, life doesn't work like that. You have to know what you want, work out where you are, then figure out how to get there.

Where do you think you sit on Maslow's Hierarchy of Needs at the moment? Why do you think that is? Complete the sentence in the box below.

For example:

I think I am at the *Esteem* **level of Maslow's Hierarchy of Needs because** *all of my needs from the lower sections of Maslow's are fulfilled and I have a high level of self-esteem.*

Where do your goals fit on the hierarchy? It is likely that all your goals will be motivated by at least one or more of Maslow's levels. Ask yourself why you want them and see if you can identify which needs they are trying to fulfil. In the left-hand column jot down your goals. In the right column write down which level of Maslow's they fit into. This might help you answer question 1 if you're struggling.

This should take you 5-10 minutes to complete.

Your Goals	What Level of Maslow's?

REACH FOR THE STARS

"We are all in the gutter, but some of us are looking at the stars."
Oscar Wilde

Whether it be Oscar Wilde or S Club 7, reaching for the STARS is a sign of optimism and positivity, which we control with our mindset.

I touched on Professor Carol Dweck's studies (1988) of fixed and growth mindset in my first book, but feel it is important to visit it again here because a growth mindset is integral to getting what YOU want.

For those not familiar with her work, Dweck identified the following to be typical traits and attitudes of growth and fixed mindsets.

Fixed Mindset	Growth Mindset
Avoids challenges "I don't like doing things I am not good at."	**Embraces challenges** "I know the more I practise the better I will get."
Gives up easily "I knew I couldn't do it. This is exactly why I shouldn't have tried in the first place."	**Perseveres** "Just because something is difficult it doesn't mean I should give up."
Results driven "All that work was a complete waste of time. I didn't even get what I wanted."	**Effort driven** "It may not be perfect, but I did my best, I am sure if I keep trying I will get there."
Ignores criticism "Why should I listen to them, what do they know."	**Learns from criticism** "That's really good advice, I think I will try that next time."
Threatened by others' success "It's not fair, they have everything. I bet it was handed to them on a plate, they don't know what hard work is."	**Inspired by others' success** "They work so hard, it just shows what you can achieve when you put in hard work and determination."

The view you adopt of yourself has a profound effect on the way you lead your life. It can determine whether you become the person you want to be and whether you accomplish the things you value (Dweck, 2017). Those with a fixed mindset have a deterministic view of life, they accept the cards they have been dealt as all they can ever have, in which case there is no point in striving for something more. When you think with a fixed mindset you are limiting your life, you set limits on what you can achieve. Whereas those who have a growth mindset tend to live with a greater sense of free will, they perceive the cards they have been dealt as a starting point and understand they can learn, grow and develop these into something more.

My hometown of Clydebank, just outside Glasgow, was a hub for heavy manufacturing in the shipbuilding industry up until the 1980s when most of it was moved to China and other parts of the world. During this time the area was desecrated, unemployment was high, and hope had faded. There was anger in people's veins and they were looking for someone to blame, from the factory management for shafting them or Maggie Thatcher testing her new poll tax system in Scotland, emotions were high, and mindsets were fixed.

It was also during this time my friend and namesake Alison discovered that she and her boyfriend Raymond were about to become parents. Alison at age 15 was a mere child herself and was the first teen mum in my class at school. Things have moved on over the past few decades and now having children before being married is the norm, but at the time, girls in Alison's situation were in the minority and on lots of occasions were ostracised by their peers and people in their community.

I moved away from Clydebank when I was 20 to travel the world and life before social media made it difficult to keep abreast of what your nearest and dearest family were doing, let alone your friends from school. But as the years went on, Alison often came into my thoughts, I would wonder what she was doing, how old her daughter would be and what she had made of her life. I don't know the exact statistics of how many teen parents stay together, but from what I have seen the figure is low. So my vision of Alison's journey was a life awash with challenges as a single parent.

Fast forward 20 years and you could have knocked me over with a feather when I saw a photo of Alison and Raymond on my cousin's Facebook feed. Not only were they still together but they were completely and utterly rocking it; they were married, Raymond had his own business, they had two grown-up children. One was a school teacher, the other a semi-professional football player. They had bucked the council house system and lived in a beautiful brand new house on a nice estate.

Alison and I have spoken several times about her journey, and I always reiterate how much of a hero she is to me. So many people in her situation would have settled for the council flat and free washing machine. They would have thought that life wasn't fair and that it was OK for other people as they had a better start to life. They would have talked the talk but never walked the walk. Alison is a true example of a fighter; she overcame the challenges which came her way to get what she wanted for her life. For that I commend her.

Hopefully, you can see that when it comes to achieving your own goals you need to adopt a growth mindset. If you have a fixed mindset you'll never even get off the ground. But how do you do this? And where does our mindset come from?

As I said before, when I came across the work of Professor Carol Dweck my world was blown wide open and I went on quite an emotional journey. It got me thinking about my own mindset, times in my life where it has been fixed and times where it has been growth. We all fluctuate at different stages of our lives, but I think I can fairly say I have managed to live my life primarily with a growth mindset. I have always wanted to reach for the stars and had the self-belief to go for it. I started to question why this was. Where did I get this sense of tenacity and determination from?

Thinking back to my childhood, my parents had always rewarded me for effort. As the youngest of two, I think they always hoped

I was going to follow in my big sister's footsteps; she has always been an academic and passed her O-grade (similar to GCSEs) and Highers (similar to A-levels) with flying colours. However, being an undiagnosed dyslexic put a stop to that, I hated school and the very thought of exams made my stomach churn. Throughout my school life, it became clear to my parents that perhaps academia wasn't for me. Finally, when it came to O-grade results day there was only one positive result on the certificate, a C for arithmetic. Was I berated for poor results? Far from it. The house was full of cards and flowers from my extended family congratulating me on my efforts.

My parents had never judged me on my grades, they saw the hard work I put in and had total belief that I did my best. Looking back at my teenage self, who would have thought that being seen as the less academic one would actually be a positive and benefit me throughout my life? The fact that I was never rewarded on my grades meant that I have never been afraid to fail, which cultivated my growth mindset.

There is a point in almost every person's life when they will get sucked into a fixed way of thinking; for some this might only last a short period of time, and for others, they get stuck in it for longer. Negative statements like, "I can't do that, I'm not good at that", "Life's not fair, that's just how it is", "I tried that and it didn't work, there's no point in trying again", or "it's all right for them, they don't even have to try!" are all examples of fixed mindset. These defeatist statements are bounced around all the time as excuses as to why people are not getting what they want. The challenges of 2020 have pushed even the highest growth mindsets to the limit at times.

How do you go from a fixed to a growth mindset? Is it even possible? Is it really that easy to just jump from one way of thinking to another? First of all, yes, it is possible, and secondly, no I don't believe it is that easy. I think like anything it takes time and practice. As I said previously, you will fluctuate through the two mindsets throughout life, this is what we call the mixed mindset. Looking back at our buddy Maslow's Hierarchy of Needs, this is why we move up and down the levels throughout our lives. When we are thinking with a growth mindset we develop and often move up the ranks towards self-actualisation, but when we fall back into the trap of thinking with a fixed mindset we take a step backwards or get stuck at the same level unable to progress.

There will be moments in your life that you will be able to look back on and clearly identify whether you were operating under a fixed or growth mindset, and other times the line can be incredibly blurry. I think it's possible to adopt both mindsets at the same time in your life but in different aspects. For example, you might go through your working day under a fixed mindset, unable to see any positives, whereas the moment you leave work and go to football practice with your team, you adopt a growth mindset, seeing the potential for your team to win the league trophy if you keep running drills and practising.

But how do you make the change from a fixed to a growth mindset? According to Dweck (2017) one of the key ingredients to making the switch is actually learning about the growth mindset and how the brain works. Science shows that the brain is malleable and the connectivity can change between neurons over time depending on your experiences. The more you do something, the more you practise tasks, the neural network grows new connections, which becomes stronger and impulse transmissions become faster. Your everyday actions and experiences increase your neural growth. Basically what this means is your brain grows.

A study by Good et al (2003) demonstrates how those who are taught about a growth mindset generally perform better. Students headed for college were divided into groups and provided with mentors. Some of the students were taught about the growth mindset and how their brain works, whereas the other students were taught about the safety around alcohol and drugs as they head into college. Those who learned about the science of the brain and growth mindset showed a bigger improvement in their test scores than those who didn't. This supports Dweck's theory that awareness of mindset and understanding of the brain plays a large part in adopting a growth mindset.

This is great news for you. By picking up this book and getting stuck in you have already taken the first steps towards switching mindsets. For some this will be enough and you'll hit the ground running, but for others you might need more information and knowledge around the brain, how it works, and what it does. There is a reason for this, but we will get on to that later. If you would like to know more about the science and psychology behind mindset, I highly recommend reading Dweck's book *Mindset: Changing The Way You Think To Fulfil Your Potential.*

Think about your own personal experiences and try to think about some times where things either didn't go how you wanted or went better than you thought. Try to identify times in your life where you have been using a fixed or growth mindset and what the outcome of this thinking was. In the left-hand column jot down the situation. In the centre column identify whether you were using a fixed or growth mindset. Finally, in the right-hand column write down what the outcome from this situation was.

This should take you 5-10 minutes

The Situation	Fixed Or Growth Mindset?	The Outcome

The Big Wave

I love the sea and have always referred to it as 'the place where it all makes sense'. Thankfully, I have been blessed to have visited some of the world's finest beaches in Cape Town, Sydney, L.A., Hawaii, Dubai, and of course, I can't forget the banks of the River Clyde!

One of my favourite things is an early morning swim. I love the way the saltwater tingles on my skin, invigorating me and making me feel alive. It has always helped me to feel present and clear my thoughts.

When I started travelling; my original plan was to move to Cape Town for a year, then return home to Scotland. However, I soon discovered a thirst for exploring new places. Very quickly the year had disintegrated and before I knew it what was supposed to be 12 months had become six years. By the end of my adventure, I was sick and tired of living out of my backpack, I missed my family and knew it was time to return home.

I have always been one to make a grand entrance, and this time would be no different. I was determined to look better than ever. In preparation for the prodigal daughter to return, I had been working hard to achieve the best tan of my life. I had also paid a visit to the salon and had my nails polished to perfection, long, red and shiny. I was looking fantastic, even if I do say so myself. My excitement was through the roof, I couldn't wait to get back home and show everyone the new and improved me.

Well, that was the case until I came face to face with the BIG WAVE! The morning of my flight I decided to visit the beach one last time before heading to the airport; after all, it was December, the height of the summer season in Australia but freezing cold in the UK. The water did not disappoint, it was clean and clear but my mind was distracted with the thoughts of the 24-hour flight, who I was going to see, and what I was going to do when I got home. I paddled through the waves, one stroke at a time, lost in my own world of thoughts.

I had made the mistake of becoming complacent in Mother Nature and did not realise the change in the ocean. I was happily paddling along when I had that feeling, you know that sort of prickly feeling you get when you have your back to the room and you can feel someone's eyes on you. That feeling of a sixth sense. I looked up and that's when I saw it approaching. It was coming at me thick and fast. It was as though a wall of water was rushing towards me getting bigger and bigger the closer it got. I was so distracted I had not seen it on the horizon. At that moment all I could feel was fear rushing through my body.

You may be familiar with the concept of fight, flight or freeze. It was originally described by Walter Cannon in the 1920s and has since been explored by Prof Steve Peters in his fantastic book *The Chimp Paradox*. When humans experience danger, the brain reverts to its natural instincts, as it would in caveman times. This drives you to fight, flight or freeze. You can see how this links to the security level of Maslow's Hierarchy of Needs. This was my exact reaction when I saw the big wave! My brain had registered that I was in danger and the alarm bells in my head had started ringing, my heart rate and blood pressure had increased and the adrenaline was rocketing through my veins.

My protection instincts had kicked in and my survival was the only thing that mattered. I could fight which would mean ducking under the wave and hoping it washed over the top of me, or I could rely on my flight response, which would have meant turning around and trying to outswim the wave back to shore. However, I did neither of these things. Sometimes when faced with overwhelming fear, our body doesn't know whether to fight or flight, so instead it freezes, like a rabbit caught in the headlights. This is what I did, I froze unable to move as I watched the huge wave come crashing down on top of me.

Like a pair of odd socks in a washing machine, the wave swallowed me whole. It pulled me under the water and sent me tumbling around and around, pinning me down and dragging me across the ocean floor. As the wave sent my body spiralling so did my mind. Memories came crashing back at 100mph, my family, my friends, it was as though my whole life flashed before my eyes. What was in reality only a matter of seconds felt like forever as I was tossed and turned under the water, not knowing which way was up and which way was down. My mind raced as I struggled to locate the surface.

Eventually, like a toddler spitting out their vegetables, the ocean spat me back out on to the shore. It was like a scene from *Bridget Jones's Diary*, my hair wasn't so much Malibu Barbie as it was Edward Scissorhands. While I had been washed up on the sand, my bikini top was making its own way home. I stood there, rooted to the spot in utter shock, trying to catch my breath. My bikini bottoms at my feet, covered in grazes from the gritty sand, and my nails, my precious perfectly manicured nails, they were chipped and jagged, broken to the quick. Fellow sunbathers and beachgoers watched me with amusement, laughing their heads off as I struggled to pull myself together. Not only was it embarrassing at that moment, but I knew that when I returned home to Scotland, instead of looking like the travelling goddess I had hoped for, I would resemble the victim of a car crash.

After this incident it would have been very easy for me to have avoided going in the sea, it would be easy to say 'never again!' and watch the glistening waves from afar. But I have always loved the beach, would I be content with never going in the ocean again out of fear for another big wave? No, I would not! I would not let the fear hold me back. I still go in the sea and I still love it, although I have learned my lesson to not let Mother Nature's calming sense of serenity lull me into a false sense of security. I swim and have fun in the same way I always have, but now I make sure to respect the ocean the way it deserves.

You see, the big wave is a lot like life. Throughout life there will be things that catch you off guard and turn you upside down, making you question everything you thought you knew. 2020, the year of the world pandemic, has had this effect on a lot of people's lives. One minute we were watching TV reports from China, the next thing we were locked up in our homes for months only being allowed out for one hour per day to exercise. COVID-19 was the tsunami of big waves.

Whether it be a pandemic, a break-up, losing a loved one or something as small as failing an exam, sometimes things happen that are out of our control and they throw you completely off course. When you have experienced fear or emotional turmoil it's easy to slip into the fixed mindset and let the big wave hold you back. But we all know that this won't get you anywhere in the long term. The fixed mindset uses fear as a weapon, the fear of rejection, the fear of embarrassment, the fear of failing, the fixed mindset latches on to these feelings. Bringing it back to the brain, this is a form of self-defence, but in reality, these things are nothing to be afraid of, fear is just another hurdle holding you back from getting what you really want.

One of the key things that I took from analysing my experience with the big wave is that the aim isn't to control or banish the fight, flight or freeze response but work with it and manage it. I think this is the same approach to take when switching mindsets. Attempting to remove all existence of a fixed mindset is impossible, there's always going to be times in your life where you're caught off-guard and the fixed mindset takes over, sneaking in like a thief in the night. Fear is natural, it's there to keep us safe, but don't let your fixed mindset use it as a weapon against you. You can't just ignore the fixed mindset and try to arm wrestle it into submission, it just isn't that easy. Instead, you need to acknowledge it, accept it and try to work with it.

SMASH IT! Model

There are thousands of models and processes out there that promise to hold the secret of turning a fixed mindset into growth. Without a map or, today, Google Maps, it's difficult to reach your destination. Without a model to follow, it becomes difficult to get back on the horse when you fall off. Think about it like building a piece of flat-pack furniture. If you follow the instructions, you'll end up with the finished article. If you don't, you end up with a wobbly table and seven extra homeless screws! My SMASH IT! model is your guide to getting what YOU want. If things don't go the way you hope, you can identify exactly where you fell off, and how to get back on.

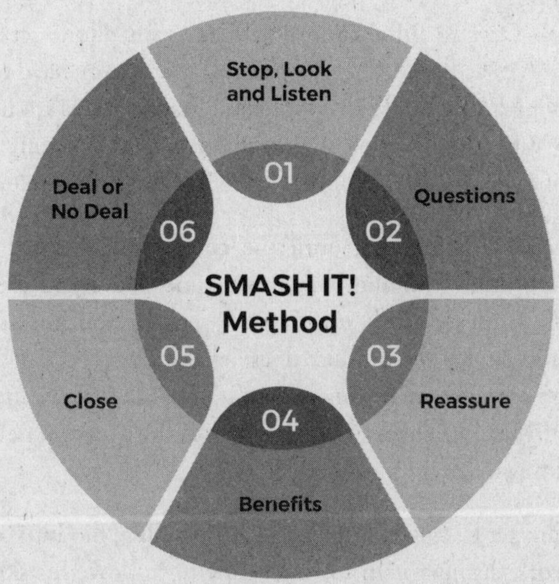

As an example of how you can use my SMASH IT! method to get what YOU want, let's look at the story of Matt. Matt is a 19-year-old high street retail worker. The store he works in is an electrical retailer which stocks thousands of products and new lines are being added all the time. Matt's goal is to be accepted onto the retailer management programme within 12 months, which means he will receive a 20% pay rise, be in the running for potential bonuses and additional paid holiday.

The reason he wants to earn more money is so he can go on holiday with his friends to Ibiza. All of his friends went last year but Matt couldn't afford to go and he can't face another year subject to the 'Ibiza 2019 highlights reel' on his pal's Instagram and the "when we were in Ibiza" stories every time they get together. This year Matt is determined to join his friends on the ultimate Ibiza party holiday, he even has a 'Days to Ibiza' countdown set as his phone screensaver. Matt still lives at home with his parents and doesn't have to worry about paying the bills. He is a popular colleague at work, known for his witty WhatsApp banter. A promotion would not only mean a holiday of a lifetime in Ibiza but also boost his self-esteem.

Everything was going well until the company had asked him to do online product training in his own time. Have you ever asked a question in an electrical store and the salesperson knows almost nothing about what the product does, let alone why it's any better or worse than a similar one sitting next to it? You can see how important it is to aid Matt's chances to be accepted to the programme that his product knowledge is up to scratch.

Matt's manager has given him access to the online modules and told him to work through it in his own time to improve his skills. The company is a great one to work for, with higher pay rates than other stores and when you become a manager, the perks are outstanding and employees receive top-end gadgets for free. There is only one fly in the ointment: it has a policy that personal development is not paid for, but his boss is sure it will improve his chances of getting one of the well sought after spaces on the course.

The voice in our head is *very powerful* and sometimes tells us completely irrational things. Let's look at how by using the SMASH IT! method, we can help Matt get what he wants.

Step 1 – Stop, Look and Listen

The first step is to listen to the voice, no I don't mean tune into Will.I.AM and Tom Jones on the Saturday night TV show *The Voice*, I mean listen to the one that sits between your two ears. Learn to recognise your fixed mindset and what it says; once you're able to identify it and how it works, it will become easier to pick up on it and identify when it's taken over.

Like Matt, we all have them. The voice in Matt's head is telling him that he wants the promotion but he will not do the self-development in his own time. The fixed mindset is shouting in his ear, 'If you want me to do anything, you need to pay me! I don't know why I'm bothering to go for a promotion anyway, I probably won't get it. I'm just going to tell them to stick it and get another job!... I'm really worried, I'm not very good at online learning, what if I get them all wrong and they think I'm stupid? What if the lads at work think I'm stupid? They will laugh at me.'

Thinking back to the characteristics of fixed and growth mindsets that we discussed in the table earlier, you can see Matt has a fear of failure and is thinking only about whether he passes or fails. This tells us that Matt is results driven, and the fear of not getting the result he wants means he is trying to avoid the challenge, giving up before he's even started, all of which are signs of a fixed mindset.

Think back to a time when you reacted to a situation with a fixed mindset. Think about the kind of thoughts you had, what was the little voice in your head saying to you? Jot these thoughts down in the box below.

This should take you three minutes to complete.

What My Fixed Mindset Voice Sounds Like

Step 2 – Questions

The second step in the SMASH IT! method is to use open questioning techniques to find the root of the objection. Interrogate the voice, ask it the open questions to find the source of the fixed thoughts. Remember an open question is one that starts with who, what, when, where, why and how.

Going back to Matt, this is when he needs to start challenging the voice in his head. Asking himself:

- Why shouldn't I do the learning in my own time?
- Why am I worried about failing?
- What makes you think you're not good at online learning?
- What is the worst that can happen if my colleagues laugh at me?
- How does this affect my chances of getting on to the retailer management programme?
- What does this mean in terms of my holiday to Ibiza?

Using the box below I want you to write down five open questions that you can ask yourself when you identify that a fixed mindset is in play. Try to keep your questions focused and targeted on what the voice in your head is telling you; be prepared, broad questions like 'why do I feel like this?' can send you down a rabbit hole of emotion, thinking about your past, and perpetuate feelings of blame which only reinforce a fixed mindset.

This should take you 5-10 minutes to complete.

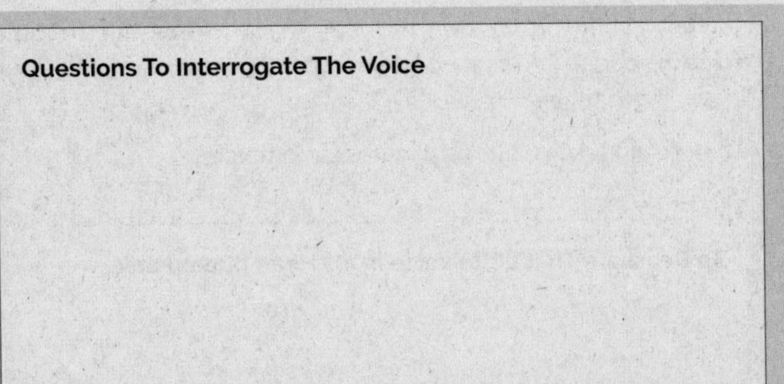

Step 3 – Reassure

You need to reassure the little voice in your head, let it know that it's OK to have these feelings, they are perfectly normal. Like I said before, the fixed mindset stems from that part of your brain that wants to keep you safe and alive, the voice in your head just wants to protect you, it doesn't mean to hold you back.

At this point Matt should be saying to himself, 'It's OK, I know you think you should be getting paid for the training, but this is the first time they have asked you to do something like this, it's not going to happen all the time. Online learning might seem a little scary at first but you already know a lot about the products, you sell them all the time. You are already halfway there, so you'll probably ace the course. And as for your colleagues, they like you for who you are. They might take the mickey for a couple of days but that will soon wear off, after all it's only a bit of banter.'

Jot down in the box below what you can say to reassure that little voice in your head. Think about your SMART goals and try to make it specific to them.

This should take you three minutes to complete..

To Reassure That Little Voice In My Head I Could Say...

Step 4 – Benefits

One of the most common mistakes people make when convincing themselves to take action is highlighting the features rather than the benefits. I always say, "Features tell and benefits sell." Let me explain the difference between the two.

Feature *- A distinctive attribute or aspect of something*

Benefit *- An advantage or profit gained from something*

If you simply point out the features, you're never going to convince yourself to take action. You need to explain how you are going to benefit from that feature. In this instance, it's important to match up the benefits of doing something to the goals you have set yourself.

This is how Matt would sell the benefits to himself: 'By investing my own time into the online course I will earn my place on the retailer management programme, the benefit of this is getting a pay rise, and the benefit of that is I can afford to go on holiday to Ibiza with my pals, and the benefit of the holiday is that I get to create my own 'Ibiza highlights reel" on Instagram.'

This is where Matt starts to shift from a fixed mindset to a growth mindset as he is able to see the benefits far outweigh the negatives. He is now ready to take on the challenge of studying the online course regardless of whether he gets paid as he can see the opportunities it holds.

Think about something in your life right now that you keep putting off, it could be anything from cleaning the kitchen cupboards to starting to plot your family tree. Write in the box whatever it is you have been avoiding and start brainstorming the different ways you will benefit from doing this.

This should take you five minutes to complete.

The Benefits Of Carrying Out This Task Are...

Step 5 – Close

For some this may be the point where you transform a fixed to a growth mindset and start taking action. For others, the voice in your head might be a little stronger than you thought and you'll need to continue with step 6.

The close is when you make the final commitment to yourself. You're not just going to talk the talk, you're going to walk the walk. It's time to go, go, go and take action!

There are three techniques you can use to close, let's use Matt to show you how this can be done:

1. **Assumptive Close** - This is a very presumptive approach and assumes you have already convinced yourself to take action. If you have followed all the steps up until this point and asked all the open questions, then the assumptive approach should be easy to do. For example, Matt would say, 'Which module will I do first?' or 'What will I set as my username on the online course?'

2. **Alternative Close** - Again this takes a presumptive approach, you are still going to do it but it gives you some flexibility around the choice as to when and how you do it. For example, Matt would say, 'When am I going to start studying, before or after my run?' or 'How should I study, on my phone or laptop?'

3. **Fear Close** - This is a classic, it uses a deadline to create an urgency to take action and build feelings of FOMO (fear of missing out). For instance, Matt would say, 'Start studying now or you won't get on to the retailer management programme, and you won't earn enough money to go on holiday with the guys this summer and you'll have to endure another year of listening to all the stories you missed out

> on.' This technique takes the benefits away from you to encourage you to take action. It's the tough love approach.

There might be times where you find that you go through each technique before you are able to convince yourself. You might start with the assumptive approach, deliver the alternative, and find you still have to go all in with the tough love, fear close.

Now it's your turn. Write down in the box an example for each of the closes to convince yourself to take action.

For example:

Assumptive Close: *Which cupboard should I clean first?*

Alternative Close: *Should I start with the pantry or the plates cupboard first?*

Fear Close: *If I don't clean the cupboards now I won't be able to put the shopping away and the kitchen will be a mess*

This should take you five minutes to complete.

My Closing Lines Are

Assumptive close

___

___

___

Alternative close

___

___

___

Fear close

___

___

___

Step 6 – Deal or No Deal

The growth mindset usually operates from a place of logic and it can usually use this to convince the fixed mindset to move on out, so it can move in. But if you still can't get that fixed voice to budge, then you need to negotiate. The key to negotiating is achieving a win-win; if you're only thinking about what you want it's not going to work, you need to think about what the voice in your head wants and reach a solution that works for you both.

If Matt had to negotiate with himself, it might sound a little bit like this:

'I know you think it's unfair that you have to study in your own time, but the pay rise you'll earn when you secure your place on the management programme will pay for the hours you put in studying. Also, you could get together with the lads at work and make a night of it, study the online course over a couple of beers, you can make it like a quiz and help each other out, it will be a laugh. It's a win-win.'

In this example you can see again how Matt's mindset is beginning to shift from fixed to growth. In some ways it looks as though he is actually looking forward to the experience. He is no longer focusing on whether he passes or fails but the experience and effort of learning new things. Subconsciously Matt is becoming aware that not only is the online course his ticket to Ibiza, but also elevates him on to the next level of Maslow's hierarchy, bringing him one step closer to self-actualisation.

The process for convincing yourself to take action and overcome internal objections is a circle, as you can see from the diagram. This is because you won't always convince yourself the first time, you might have to go round and round before you finally make the magic happen! If Matt gets to the end of step 6 and he still hasn't logged into the online course, he needs to go back round the circle, starting at step 1. Listening is the most important part, I always say you have two ears and one mouth, use them in that order.

It's at this point that Matt needs to ask himself how much he really wants it, how strong is his WHY. Sometimes no matter how hard you try, you might not be able to strike a deal and sometimes it will be a no deal situation. This doesn't necessarily mean that you've succumbed to the pressure of the fixed mindset, but perhaps you didn't want it as much as you first thought you did, or perhaps it wasn't a SMART goal and you had unrealistic expectations. Knowing when to walk away from something that isn't right for you is as much a growth action as committing to the deal.

Use the box to practise negotiating with yourself. Think about your WHY, your goal, the benefits and what is holding you back. How can you tie all of this together to convince yourself to take growth actions? Jot down some ideas in the box below.

This should take you five minutes to complete.

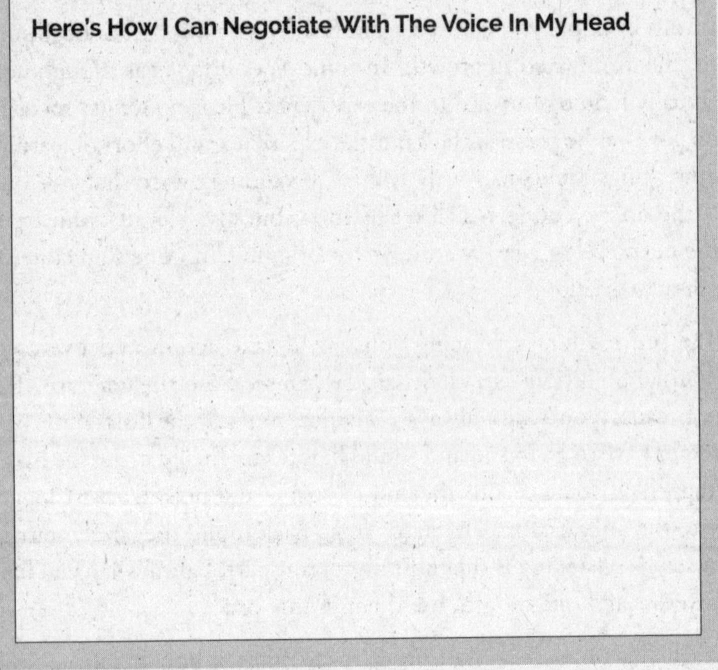
Here's How I Can Negotiate With The Voice In My Head

Practise these steps, the more you learn to recognise a fixed mindset and become comfortable talking with that little voice in your head, the easier it will become to adopt a growth mindset. The mistake so many people make is trying to just ignore the voice or push it into a dark corner. The trouble with this is that it just keeps coming back stronger and louder than a screaming toddler who doesn't get its own way! You need to deal with it, literally make a deal with it like you would if you were standing in front of Noel Edmonds and his big red boxes. The more you do this, the more comfortable it will become and at some point you'll need these steps less and less as your mind will automatically know what to do when it hears that little voice of fixed mindset.

CASE STUDY: MEET ANTHONY...

The Situation

As a young entrepreneur, Anthony started his first company at the age of 16, always dreaming of working for himself and being able to do something he loved. Following his first stint in business, he got a job in the security department at Heathrow airport as he worked on his new business White2Label. Anthony wasn't ready to give up on achieving his goals and wanted to find a way to work for himself full time.

The Problem

Being in his early 20s when he started his second business, Anthony knew that he didn't have much to lose, unlike those who started businesses later on in life when they had mortgages and families. Even though he knew this, he still couldn't find the 'right time' to make the scary leap and leave his day job to focus on his dreams full time.

The business was doing well, he was happy with its progress and actually it had become really hard to balance the business with his security job. He was running himself ragged trying to work both. And even though working in airport security wasn't his passion, it was a good steady job that he could rely on. It was something to fall back on if it all went wrong, it had become a security blanket. The only problem was, Anthony didn't need it anymore, his business was doing well, the only thing that was stopping him from living the life he really wanted was him and his fear of failing.

The Win-Win

"I thought I was too young, I didn't have a degree, I had little experience and no one in my family had ever started a business." After reading my first book, Anthony realised that the thoughts he had been having were coming from a place of fixed mindset and it was this that was holding him back. He realised that there would never be a 'right time' and that failure was nothing to be afraid of, saying, "I have made lots of mistakes and I am sure I will make many more, but I will learn from them."

Anthony had heard of growth and fixed mindsets before but never really understood what it meant. "The acknowledgement of mindset is really powerful, it's something we all have but aren't really aware of. I think the awareness of what it is and understanding how it can be changed had a detrimental effect on my life. I've always been positive but now I am more self-aware."

Now that Anthony has a clear understanding of mindset and how it can be changed, he is able to recognise when he is looking at life with a fixed mindset and follow the steps to take more positive growth actions. "The COVID-19 pandemic was a great example of this. Initially I was really worried about work slowing down and struggling financially, but then I looked at it from a growth mindset and realised it was a really good opportunity to spend time on the business in a way I haven't be able to before; we ended up having our best quarter yet."

By developing his self-awareness and understanding mindset, Anthony finally took the leap and is now living his dream, working for himself and running his business full time.

The Techniques

The key thing that Anthony was able to take from the first book was recognising what a fixed and growth mindset looked like within himself. He acknowledged any negative thoughts and rationalised they were coming from a place of fixed mindset; he would question why he felt that way and put appropriate actions to move it towards growth.

For example, when he thought about the company failing, he considered what the worst case scenario would be. He would challenge the voice in his head and realised that actually the worst thing would be that he would have to start the business again, which in his eyes wasn't the end of the world. Thinking in this way helped him to squash the irrational fears that were being fed to him by the voice in his head. All of this stems from being aware of mindset, what it means and what it looks like for you. If Anthony hadn't taken the first step and opened himself up to self-awareness, he wouldn't be living his dream today.

BEST BEHAVIOUR

Have you ever wondered why some things come so easily and others you just can't seem to figure out? Have you ever done something or said something and wondered 'why'? Do you ever look at your brothers and sisters and question how you can be so different when you share the same DNA? Yeah, me too. Lucky for you, I have the answers and I am about to share them all with you.

Knowing what motivates you is just as important as knowing what holds you back. When you understand your own behaviour and actions, you become more self-aware. This enables you to put in strategies and measures for breaking down walls that once held you back, allowing you to get the results YOU want.

Behaviour can be defined as the way in which one acts and conducts oneself, especially towards others. I think it's important to point out from the get-go that your behaviour is separate from your personality and your values. Your values are what make you who you are, these are what determine your behaviour. Driving forces and mindset also have an impact, we will discuss this in more detail as we go.

There are two key aspects when it comes to understanding behaviours: first is understanding your own, and second is understanding that of those around you. This is one of the most popular parts of my first book, so if you have read it this might sound a little familiar. However, unlike *Secrets of Successful Sales* (2018), this book is about understanding your own behaviour and how it affects getting what YOU want.

Allow me to introduce you to the DISC model. There are hundreds of theories and models used to explain human behaviour, the one I use is DISC, created by William Moulton Marston. In the 1920s whilst his peers such as Freud and Jung were focusing on the minds of criminals and psychopaths, Marston set out to explain the emotional responses of the 'normal' everyday person (Marston, 1928). Marston developed his DISC model around two assumptions:

1. Individuals consider their environment as either friendly or unfriendly.
2. Individuals consider themselves as either stronger or weaker than their external environment.

This is how Marston categorised people into introverts and extroverts.

Everybody responds differently to external factors, and how you perceive them comes back to your genetics and values, which stem back to childhood. The assumptions we make about our environment happen instinctively and quickly. It's often something we aren't even aware of. This is why it is so important to make a good first impression, as first impressions last. Marston noted four traits displayed in someone's reaction to their environment, they were (Ensize, 2019a):

1. **Dominance** - When someone tries to dominate the situation in order to achieve their goals.
2. **Influence** - When someone tries to influence others into thinking their opinions and ideas are correct.
3. **Stability** - When an individual attempts to preserve their environment and protect it from change.
4. **Compliance** - When the individual analyses the situation and follows established rules and regulations.

Dominance, Influence, Stability and Compliance come together to form DISC. Marston identified these to be the four key behavioural styles displayed by your everyday average Joe. Marston also identified them as being situational which means the behaviour someone displays can change depending on external environmental factors. Whilst you may be a manager at work and have to make tough decisions so display Dominance behaviours, at home your partner may rule the roost, so you get to sit in the passenger seat and allow them to drive, leaving you to display your true Stability behaviours.

Back to School

If you're anything like me, it may take you a while to get your head around DISC. Let me translate it into something more relatable to make it a bit easier to understand.

I don't know about you, but when I was a teenager I loved a good magazine, they were a bit of a treat in my household. I loved flicking through the pages with my pals at the bus stop, but the bit I liked the most was always the quizzes that would tell you who your celebrity boyfriend would be, or which member of your favourite girl band you were most like. I know you might be a bit young to have experienced these 'old school' type magazine quizzes, in fact you have probably never even bought a magazine now that you can get the latest celeb gossip at the swipe of your screen on your iPhones and iPads. I wouldn't want you to miss out, so I have created a quiz of my own for you to complete, unfortunately this one won't tell you which 80s heartthrob you're destined to be with!

By completing the quiz below, you'll gain a rough idea of where you sit on the DISC matrix. Don't worry if it's still a little overwhelming, I'll break it down further after the quiz.

Here are the rules:

1. Do your best to provide an answer for every question.
2. Be as honest as possible, there are no right or wrong answers.
3. You may find that you want to tick more than one answer, but try to choose the one that would represent you in most situations.
4. Try not to spend too much time thinking about your answers. This should only take you a few minutes.

The Questions

1. You've been asked to do the shopping for your elderly Granny, what's your response?

   1) No problem, I'll be in and out in 10 minutes.

   2) Sure, but it might take a while, I want to pop to a few other places while I'm out and I usually get stuck chatting to an old school pal whenever I go shopping.

   3) Of course I don't mind helping Granny. I'll put a few extra things in the basket that I think she might like. I like to make her feel happy.

4) That's fine, does Granny have a list? It says here she wants cereal, she usually gets the small box of cornflakes but the larger box is better value for money per 100g.

2. You are sending a text message to a friend you haven't seen for a while, which one of these does it most look like?

    1) Want to meet Tuesday?

    2) Hey girl, what's up? Haven't seen you forever, let's hang out soon! 😁👍

    3) Hello, I just wanted to check in and see how you were feeling this week? Xx

    4) Hello Sam, I will be in your area at 2.45 on Tuesday 15th, would you like to meet up at Ted's for a coffee to formulate a strategy for the Devizes to Westminster race?

3. You are visiting a car dealership to buy a new car after your last one broke down, what's your decision-making process?

    1) I have a few ideas of what I want, I will take it for a test drive and put down the deposit. There is no point in dragging it out.

    2) I'm not really fussed as long as it looks good on my Instagram.

    3) Buying a car is a big decision, I want something that will last. I'll have a look at my options and then think about it for a few days. I might ask my friend who knows more about cars to come with me for a second viewing.

4) I will need to look at the full specification and service history for each car. I will probably have a look at a few other dealerships to see what all my options are before making a decision.

4. You are at work and you receive a text message from your friend saying they need your advice, what do you do?

    1) I'm busy right now, I'll get back to them later.

    2) Ooooh, I wonder what it is. I reply straight away to get the gossip.

    3) I hope everything is OK, I'll send them a text message letting them know I am here if they need anything.

    4) I need some more information before I can give advice, I will call them after work to get the full story.

5. You have a job interview for a new role within your company, how do you prepare?

    1) I know all the important facts and figures, this job's got my name all over it.

    2) I know Jamie who is conducting the interview, we will probably just have a bit of a chat over coffee, no big deal.

    3) Interviews make me nervous. I have made a note of a few things to ask in case my mind goes blank and I have practised some scenarios with my colleagues just in case.

    4) I have created a portfolio outlining the job specification and how I meet the criteria, including

a detailed synopsis of my background within the company. I shall present this in the interview.

6. You have been asked to make a speech at your parents' anniversary party, how do you feel about this?

   1) I'll keep it short and sweet, throw in a few jokes and make the toast.

   2) Bring it on, I'll be great. I know how to work a crowd.

   3) Nooooo way, I do not like public speaking, maybe I can just create a nice photomontage or video instead, something that really shows their marriage throughout the years and displays their loving relationship.

   4) Speeches aren't exactly my idea of fun, I will have a chat with Mum and Dad and try to put together a timeline of their marriage. Stick to the important dates and maybe create a PowerPoint to go with it.

	A	B	C	D	TOTAL
1					
2					
3					
4					
5					

The Results

Go back over your answers and count how many times you answered A, B, C and D. Hopefully you will have a clear winner, if not don't worry, this is normal. Here's what your results mean:

Mostly As - Dominance also known as Red Behaviour

Mostly Bs - Influence also known as Yellow Behaviour

Mostly Cs - Stability also known as Green Behaviour

Mostly Ds - Compliance also known as Blue Behaviour

From here on in, to make things a little easier to digest I'll refer to the behaviour types as their corresponding colours. You can see from the cross below that I have plotted the colours to make it easier for you to visualise. Some people are task-focused whilst other people are relationship-focused. Some people are introvert, others are extrovert. By understanding where you sit on the cross, it makes it easier to understand how your behaviours affect getting what you want.

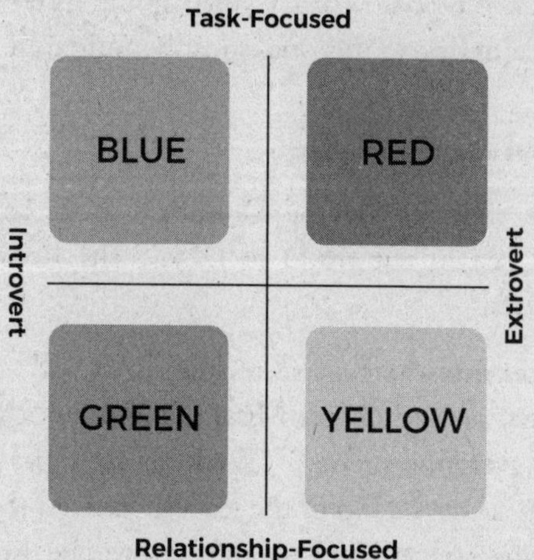

Although this offers a good baseline understanding of the behaviours, it's important to know that we shouldn't label anybody based on their dominant colour. If we label, it gives us an unconscious bias and affects how we react towards them. We are all a blend of all the colours, this will make more sense as we move through the book.

The best way for you to understand the four behaviour types is for me to take you back to school. Remember, when I am talking about the four behaviours as identified by DISC, I am talking about them in their purest forms which is why some things might sound a little extreme. It's a bit like trying to compare yourself to your favourite character from the popular TV show *Friends*. No one is ever completely Joey or Monica because they are usually written around exact stereotypes of behaviours. We are all a mix.

OK then, let's go back to school. Don't worry, I'm not going to ask you to squeeze into your old uniform or make a packed lunch.

Imagine you're sitting in a classroom. You can hear your pals whispering at the back of the room. Your teacher is standing at the front writing on the board. Today you're going to take a 30-minute English test. Calm down, this one is just hypothetical.

The Red Behaviour Types

First to finish the test are the Dominant Reds as they're more commonly known in the world of DISC. The Reds are the task-focused extroverts.

Twenty minutes into the English test the Reds will be waving their hand in the air, saying, "Miss, Miss, I've finished the test already. What's taking everyone so long?" The Reds are super confident and always strive to be at the top of the leaderboard. At this point a Red is thinking to themselves check me out, and will be using their hands to do the loser sign at all of their classmates. Does this remind you of anyone?

Being task-focused means the Reds are great at getting the task done fast, but that doesn't necessarily mean they get it right the first time. The same Red that finished the test within 20 minutes will get the paper back on results day and say, "Oh, I didn't realise there was another side to that paper." They lack attention to detail and are often more concerned with getting the task done and looking good than the actual result.

The Yellow Behaviour Types

Next, we have the Influential Yellows. They are relationship-focused extroverts.

The Yellows are the ones you can hear whispering to each other at the back of the classroom. They are easily distracted and find it difficult to stay on task, they will spend the majority of the test chatting and giggling with their pals, more concerned with the party they have been invited to at the weekend than the English test they should be completing.

When questioned by the teacher they will turn around and say, "Oops sorry Miss, I was talking to Hannah about who's going to the party at the weekend and what she's going to wear. I am going to wear my new sparkly boots with my…" Yellows could talk forever if you let them, their excitable nature along with their short attention span means they move at a very fast pace and have a tendency to take the conversation completely off topic. They are often perceived as being loud and disruptive.

The Green Behaviour Types

This brings us to the Stable Greens. These are the relationship-focused introverts.

The Greens are the quiet ones and often lack the confidence to speak up. They can come across as being quite nervous as they are often slow and hesitant to take action. Being relationship-focused, the Greens are the ones who always put others before themselves. In our classroom scenario they will be the ones to quietly usher the teacher over to whisper, "Excuse me Miss, I know we have a test but my friend Jordan has a headache and I really think I should take him to the nurse." With the permission of the teacher the Green will get up and take their friend to the nurse's office without disturbing the class, sometimes you won't even realise they've left the room.

However, Greens aren't perfect. Being relationship-focused means they may struggle to stay on task, often getting lost in their own thoughts. Even if the Green did stay for the whole test they may never have finished on time because they would spend so much time worrying over the answer to each question that they never actually finish.

The Blue Behaviour Types

Finally, we have the Compliant Blues. These are the task-focused introverts.

These will be the last ones to finish the test. Attention to detail is key for Blues, and they strive for perfection in everything they do. The Blues will be going through the test paper until the final bell goes, they utilise every minute of their time. Reviewing their answer to every question, checking that every 'i' is dotted and every 't' is crossed.

Being an introvert means the Blues would prefer to sit on their own in the corner where they can focus on the task in hand with little distraction rather than interact with the rest of the class. The Blues are sticklers for the rules and you definitely won't catch them trying to have a chat with any of their classmates throughout the test. When they get the test results back, they're likely to receive the A*, but they don't brag about their results because the only person they're trying to beat is themselves.

Living in Colour

You now have a rough overview of the four different behaviours and their basic traits. But what does this mean for you? It's really important that you start to form your self-awareness in colour because this really impacts getting what YOU want. I'm about to dive deeper into the nitty gritty of each colour to give you a better understanding. Don't worry, you don't need your scuba gear and oxygen tank. I'll keep it simple!

The Reds

Someone who has a high Red in their basic behaviour often responds to their environment with dominance. As I mentioned, Reds are task-focused extroverts. As someone who is task-focused, Reds like to get things done and face challenges head on. When it comes to obstacles they are quick to make decisions and solve the problem in order to get back on track. The extrovert in them means they are confident, outspoken and not afraid to take charge.

As natural leaders, a high Red will often be the Queen Bee of the social group or leader of the pack. They are the ones who make all the plans and get everyone together, sometimes coming across as controlling. They are so focused on getting things done their own way that they struggle to listen to the opinions and ideas of those around them, a bit like a bull in a china shop.

As one myself, I always say there are two things we high Reds need to be aware of: there is a thin line between assertive and aggressive, and a thin line between confident and cocky; someone who is a high Red doesn't always know where those lines are.

Each behaviour style has positive and negative attributes. As I said before, everyone has their good and bad days. Your mindset, along with your values and driving forces (we'll come back to these later), will impact how you respond to a situation. For example, on a good day with a growth mindset, someone who possesses high Red behaviour will be seen as resilient and overcome hurdles to push forward. Whereas on a bad day with a negative mindset, a high Red will let their fear of failure take over; thinking they know best, they will ignore any advice from those around them. To make it easier for you I have divided typical Red traits into two groups – growth and fixed. It's likely that on a bad day you'll be displaying fixed traits compared to on a good day when you will be exhibiting more growth traits. The table below helps to break this down further.

Fixed Traits	Growth Traits
Fear of failure	Takes on challenges
Dislikes criticism	Problem solver
Impatient	Embraces change
Single-minded	Determined
Controlling	Decisive
Bossy	Leadership skills
Stubborn	Tenacious

At this point you should have a fairly good understanding of what the behaviour of someone who is a high Red will look like. But how do you recognise these within yourself? It's time to take an inward glance and be completely honest with yourself. Below I have listed some statements, tick the ones you agree with. This should reiterate the quiz result and allow you to see your balance of colours as you work through the sections. If you find that you agree with the majority of them, then you are most probably a high Red. Remember there is nothing wrong with being a Red, Yellow, Green or Blue, they all have strengths and weaknesses, the important thing is to identify what you are so you can become more self-aware and use this to your own advantage.

- I feel satisfied when I am recognised for my achievements
- I feel satisfied when I am viewed as a leader and have authority
- I feel satisfied when things happen in a timely manner
- I feel satisfied when I win something
- I feel satisfied when I get to cross something off my to-do list
- I feel frustrated when people procrastinate and waste my time
- I feel frustrated when I don't know how to do things
- I feel frustrated when those around me challenge my opinion instead of trusting me
- I feel frustrated when someone is late for something
- I feel frustrated when those around me are indecisive

If like me you are a high Red then you might consider yourself a bit of a goal smasher. If this is the case, then why do you still feel like you're not getting what you want? I am going to share with you how being a high Red might be holding you back more than you thought and what you can do to overcome these setbacks.

Someone who is a Red knows what they want and isn't afraid to go for it. Determination is a great quality to have, but for a Red it can also be the thing that holds them back. They are often so laser-focused on achieving their goals and ticking another one off the list that it becomes a case of quantity over quality. Sometimes you can be so focused on the task and making sure that it gets done that you forget why you wanted it in the first place. Can you think of a time when this happened in your life? I can certainly think of a few. When you get there you realise that in a bid to smash your goal you settled for second best, which means you're no further forward than when you started. Try as you might to convince yourself you got what you wanted, deep down you know that is not the case and you're left thinking what could have been, if only you had stayed true to yourself.

One of the reasons a Red does this is because as much as they love a challenge, the thought of failure annoys them, so they try to complete their goals whatever the cost. Reds are competitive (even when it means competing with themselves) and want to show they are in charge, that they own the situation.

The mistake many Reds make when they set goals is ignoring the SMART system. Being specific is the enemy for a Red, they avoid it like the plague. The more specific you are, the more criteria you set, the bigger the risk of failure. Keeping goals vague makes them easier to achieve. But as you already know, there is a reason the SMART system exists; when you are specific it makes you think about what you really want and keeps you on plan. When you're not, you end up chasing something that is so far from what you imagined when you set your goals that when you do come to ticking it off, you are left feeling unsatisfied and yearning for more.

Time is another enemy that holds back those who are Red. Being task-focused extroverts means they are impatient, when they want something they want it **now**! I can guarantee you that any Red you know will be the proud owner of an Amazon Prime subscription, ensuring they don't have to wait any longer than necessary to receive their goods. If something is taking too long to achieve, they will start looking for the shortcuts, as they become more concerned about being able to say they've done it than actually doing it. This means long-term goals are really difficult for Reds as they will just trade it in for something they can have here and now, convincing themselves: why would I want that long-term goal when I can do this now? But because they move at a fast pace, they'll soon forget all about that short-term gain and be wishing they stuck it out to get what they really wanted.

At this point you should be thinking about the goals you set at the beginning of the book. Did you complete the SMART task? Be honest now, did you skip the tasks because you thought you could get to the end of the book quicker if you didn't do them? If yes, then now is when you need to go back to the beginning and do things properly. I know this is difficult but it really is a short-term pain for long-term gain.

Break it down! I cannot say this enough. If you recognise yourself as a Red then you already know that long-term commitment to goals is tough for you. You need to break down those long-term goals into short-term milestones that you can use to keep focused. For Reds it really is about celebrating the smaller daily achievements. When you do this, the task-focused part of you is still satisfied and the craving for task completion is suppressed. Reds love affirmation, giving yourself a pat on the back or a virtual high five will fulfil this need and stop you from trying to zoom over the finish line before you're ready. Which ultimately helps you move forward to getting what you really want.

To recap, my top tips to help you get what you want if you display Red behaviour:

1. Be SMART - The system exists for a reason, use it as intended and it will help keep you on track to achieve what you really want, not want right now.
2. Break it down - Being task-focused means you are impatient, so break down the big goals into smaller daily and weekly ones.
3. Celebrate the little wins - As a Red you seek gratification, celebrate the everyday changes and achievements as this will stop you from trying to rush to the finish line.

The Yellows

Those who have high Yellow behaviour use the power of influence to respond to a situation. Like the Reds, the Yellows are extroverts too, but they are relationship-focused rather than task-focused. This means that instead of dominating tasks and proving to their peers they are the best, they prefer to focus on changing the minds of those around them by influencing them into their way of thinking.

Being extroverts, Yellows love attention and they are known for being loud and disruptive. Yellows want the whole world to revolve around them and the best way of doing this is by making sure you always know when they are in the room. It's not just that Yellows want to be the centre of attention, they are considered as inspiring and motivational to their friends and family and are thrust into the limelight by them. However, this does mean that they don't always respond well to criticism, as subconsciously they feel they have failed to influence the situation and perceive the criticism as an environmental threat.

Yellows can be very persuasive which makes them great at enlisting others into help, it also means they are great at bringing different people together. The combination of being relationship-focused and an extrovert results in a high energy that can't help but attract everything and everyone in its surroundings. However, this high energy can sometimes come off as being frantic and flaky. Their excitable nature means they are easily distracted and can have so many plates spinning that they struggle to keep them all in the air.

Someone who is high Yellow will rely a lot on their intuition, acting and reacting based on their feelings and gut instincts rather than on facts and figures. As a result, they are not afraid to break the rules in order to get what they want, seen as a bit of a free spirit or risk taker.

Looking to the media for an example, I can't think of anyone better than Will Smith. Ever since his early days in the industry he has always been a big character, displaying high Yellow behaviour. He is always loud and animated, playing the joker. If you have ever seen him appear on a television chat show, you'll know he has an undeniable presence. Without trying, he becomes the main focus of the show; despite other guests who might also be appearing, he still manages to steal the limelight. He is a natural entertainer, effortlessly winning over the audience and charming them. Not only that but he has his fingers in many pies so to speak, he doesn't stick to one industry, he goes from television, to music, to film and back again. He is always changing things up to keep it exciting and fresh, a typical sign of someone with high Yellow behaviour.

Now, the Yellows may seem all rainbows and sunshine but that is not always the case. Sure, there are the good days where their energy is either infectious or annoying, depending on the people they are in the room with, and they are without a doubt the bubbliest person in every room. But there are also the darker days, when they feel overwhelmed with a hundred million things going on, it feels like everything is spinning out of control. Let's take a closer look at the fixed and growth traits within Yellow behaviour.

Fixed Traits	Growth Traits
Erratic	Energetic
Overwhelmed	Multitasker
Unrealistic	Optimistic
Easily distracted	Adaptable
Careless	Intuitive
Self-centred	Team builder
Materialistic	Creative
Bad listener	Strong verbal communicator

As you know, I am a high Red. It is normal for most people to have two dominant behaviours; if you have not already guessed it, Yellow is my other dominant behaviour. I am well known in my world for being the bubbly Scottish woman in pink. Like before, read through the statements below and tick the ones you agree with. If you find you agree with the majority of the following statements, then it's more than likely that Yellow is one of your dominant behaviour styles too.

- I am happy when I am in the spotlight
- I am happy when I can spend my time with people
- I am happy when my work is fun
- I am happy when people like my ideas and opinions
- I am happy when I have lots of different things to do
- I am annoyed when I have to do the same thing over and over again
- I am annoyed when there are too many rules and regulations to follow

- I am annoyed when I have to do things that are boring
- I am annoyed when my friends do things without me
- I am annoyed when people don't remember me

A nickname I have always given the Yellows is half-a-job Harry. They are great at starting tasks and setting new goals but not so good when it comes to finishing them. Sometimes the Yellows struggle to deposit into their Banks of Balance in the right order – they tend to deposit in the Bank of Faffing Around. This is because, unlike the Reds, they prioritise relationships and social interaction over tasks. This is where someone like me who is a high Red and high Yellow might experience some internal conflict. The Red in you craves goal achievement but the Yellow in you is always too distracted to finish the task in hand, always starting on the next thing before the first is complete.

As I mentioned, Yellows are relationship-focused extroverts, people are what inspire and motivate you. You don't want to be sitting alone at your desk whilst your pals are off having fun, so get them involved where you can. Use your strength as an influencer and team builder to build an environment that encourages you to stay on task and keep focused. You are more likely to do something if it means a chance to hang out with your friends at the same time. Whether your goal is to lose weight, learn a language or get a promotion, look for ways you can incorporate others. This way it will be much more fun, not only will it help to keep you focused on your goal but also meet the needs for social interaction at the same time. However, I will warn you now, if your social group is made up of too many Yellows this will only cause more distraction, try to incorporate friends who have a different behaviour from you.

This comes back to the Love and Belonging section of Maslow's Hierarchy of Needs. This is why the relationship-focused behaviour types (Yellow and Green) have found the COVID-19 pandemic particularly difficult. They weren't able to interact with their friends, family and wider community in the ways they wanted to. Virtual air kisses have nowhere near as much impact as big bear hugs.

Another major hurdle a Yellow faces is losing sight of their WHY. It is easy to flit from one goal to the next when you're not really sure why you want something. When it came to writing my books my WHY was always strong, hence no matter how distracted I was I knew it was something I wanted to finish. But what about when your WHY isn't strong?

Yellows can sometimes be considered materialistic, placing too much importance on status symbols and prestige objects. Any of the four behaviours could be materialistic, but it is more popular for those who have high Yellow behaviour. Someone who is a Yellow will automatically try to influence their surroundings, it's their natural defence. Much like social media when someone is seen as an 'influencer' because they have the branded merch or flash whip, their followers want it. A Yellow will do what they have to in order to become the most influential person in the room, even if that means purchasing a designer bag or investing in a pair of trainers worth more than a month's salary. But it doesn't always leave them feeling fulfilled.

I have fallen into this trap myself. Every business year I start off by setting a big goal that I want to achieve; 2015 was the year of the Jaguar. I wanted to earn enough money to buy myself a new flash car that I could drive around in. Why? Because the other people in my industry had been posting pictures of their flash new motors and everyone thought it was great. I wanted to be seen as a success too, therefore I would need a new car to boast about on social media. I achieved my goal and by the end of the year managed to bag myself a brand-new white Jaguar XF. I was going to look the part when I rolled up at my next meeting or social event, hell I would look great at the supermarket in this car!

Years later and I hate driving my car as much as the day I bought it; I never thought about what it would actually be like to drive, I was just thinking how sleek and stylish it looked. Parking is an absolute nightmare; it has a big nose and a huge backside (just like me!) and even with sensors it is never easy to park. Not only that, but it turns out I don't actually care what people think of my car. Driving around in it makes me feel no different than if I were driving around in my old Kia.

For the Yellows, it's especially important to know your WHY as they can often be distracted by the 'shiny objects'. If you don't know WHY you set your goal it will result in one of two ways. The first is that you won't even see the goal out because you will find something more interesting to distract you. The second outcome is that if you do actually manage to achieve the goal, you'll be left feeling unsatisfied and regret wasting your time on trying to achieve it. Like me with the Jaguar XF, Yellows often set goals for the wrong reason, aiming for things because other people want them. You're reading this book because you want to get what YOU want, not what anyone else wants.

Go back to the goals you set at the beginning and really analyse what you've written down. A bit like we did in the overcoming objections section, interrogate yourself and find out why you set this goal. Use the open questioning techniques. Why do you really want it? Maybe you want it because someone else has it or maybe you can't explain why you want it at all; if so there is a good chance you don't want it as much as you first thought you did.

Use Maslow's Hierarchy of Needs to help guide you, think about where you currently sit and how this might be impacting your decision to set certain goals. Perhaps like me you have set a materialistic goal, which there is absolutely nothing wrong with if you have set it for the right reasons. What are the right reasons? Well that's entirely up to you, trust your gut, you are a Yellow after all.

If you want to buy a five-bedroom house because it will make a great family home one day and you can see your kids growing up there and spending summers in the garden, fantastic, go for it! But if you want to buy a five-bedroom house because it's impressive and shows you're earning great money, then maybe when you finally move in, it will actually feel bigger and emptier than you thought, and you'll miss your two-bed apartment in the city centre. Yellows rush into things at full speed, take a minute to stop and think first.

To summarise my top tips for the Yellows to help them get what they want:

1. Know your WHY - Always know why you want something. If your WHY is strong you can't go wrong.
2. Make goals inclusive - You are relationship-focused, use your skills as a team builder and get your pals involved where you can.
3. Keep it fun - You are easily distracted, try to find the fun in everything you do and keep goal-related tasks short and snappy where possible.

The Greens

People showing Green behaviour desire stability and therefore seek ways to feel safe and secure within their environment. This means they are good when it comes to following rules and sticking to plans, however they are not so good at adapting to change. Greens prefer to live by the 'if it's not broke, don't fix it' approach. They feel safe and secure when their environment is familiar, change can throw them off balance. More often than not, someone who is high in Green will try to maintain the status quo whenever they can.

They are relationship-focused like the Yellows, but where they differ is that the Greens are introverts. The combination of the two results in someone who is warm and friendly, people feel at home and welcome in their presence. When a Green first meets someone new they will usually wait for the other person to initiate conversation, a lack of confidence can hold them back from making the first move. However, once comfortable they are kind and talkative. Greens are great listeners, taking on board everyone's ideas and opinions without judgment. They are the type of friend you trust to confide in and turn to when you need advice. Unlike extroverts who want to be known by everyone, the introvert in Greens means they prefer to build more meaningful long-lasting relationships, for them it's about quality over quantity.

Known for being the peacekeepers, someone who is a Green will do their best to avoid any animosity. Very rarely would a Green be at the centre of any conflict, but on the odd occasion that it does happen they are known for being able to diffuse the situation and bring about a calming atmosphere. Always doing their best to stabilise the environment and protect it from upheaval and change.

A high Green will always think before they speak, taking their time to make decisions and think about all the possible outcomes of their choices. When making decisions, the Greens need more time than others, they tend to be quite indecisive and struggle when forced to make decisions on their own. This is due to a lack of confidence. Someone who has Green as their dominant behaviour style will need reassurance and confirmation from their peers that they are doing the right things as they often doubt their capabilities and their worth.

Being relationship-focused, the Greens are great at cooperating with others. They are the people pleasers, always wanting to make the people around them happy, doing what they can to provide support. As a result, they struggle to say no, which can land them in some sticky situations and leaves them feeling overwhelmed. Their inability to turn someone down means the Greens will often find themselves agreeing to things they don't really want.

It's difficult to find an example of a high Green in the media; being an introvert they wouldn't usually choose to spend time in the limelight, instead opting for more supportive roles.

When learning about the Greens it seems as though they almost give off an air of serenity, they are gentle and kind, it's hard to imagine them losing control. But of course it happens, they are not perfect, they are human after all. Someone with Green behaviour doesn't lose their temper a lot, the majority of the time when they feel angry they will retreat from the situation but there are times when their emotions get the better of them.

When a Green gets riled up it's something they're not sure how to deal with, the combination of anxiety, confusion and heightened emotions, it's like the cork popping out of a champagne bottle. If you ever witness a Green at this point, you might misinterpret them for a bad day Red. The only problem is that once the cork has been popped, it can't go back on and a Green will hold a grudge against the person or thing that caused them to pop.

Now, let's take a closer look at the fixed and growth traits of a Green behaviour.

Fixed Traits	Growth Traits
Indecisive	Thoughtful
Resistant to change	Drives stability
Quiet	Good listener
Dependent on others	Cooperative
Anxious	Well organised
Self-doubt	Supportive of others
Lacks confidence	Considerate
Guarded	Loyal

As I have said before, we are a mix of all the behaviours, some are just higher than others. We are all different combinations. Read through the statements below and tick the ones you agree with; if it is more than half, then you most probably have a high level of Green behaviour.

- I am content when I am in a familiar and safe environment
- I am content when I have the support of those around me
- I am content when I can plan for the future
- I am content when there are guidelines and instructions to follow
- I am content having the same routine every day
- I am uncomfortable when I have to do something I have never done before
- I am uncomfortable when I have to make last-minute changes to my plans
- I am uncomfortable when I meet new people
- I am uncomfortable when I have to be spontaneous or improvise
- I am uncomfortable when I have to visit new places by myself

I know what you're thinking, if the Greens are so good at long-term planning then what is the problem? Allow me to enlighten you. The Greens are known for having the patience of a saint, but it's actually this quality that can sometimes hold them back. Unlike the Reds and Yellows, the Greens don't seek instant gratification and are actually really good when it comes to planning for the future and setting long-term goals. However, they are not so good when it comes to putting those plans into action. Their naturally patient approach to life means they can be rather relaxed when it comes to getting started and what started out as a five-year goal can end up taking 25 years, taking the 'good things come to those who wait' approach a little too far.

The way to overcome this is by setting stricter time schedules. Break down your goals into smaller steps using Alison Edgar's Big Balls to help you. I have no doubt that as a Green you would have followed the instructions and completed the tasks. I want you to review the SMART goals you set yourself. I am sure that you followed the SMART system but I have a feeling that most of the goals you would have set yourself are long-term goals. What about now? A fear of change along with an incredible ability to be patient means that you avoid setting short-term goals that could alter your life before you're ready.

Guess what? You are ready! By picking up this book you have shown that you are open and willing to make the changes required to SMASH IT! Grab the bull by the horns and start getting what you want **now**! Not next month or next year. It's the Time-based aspect of SMART which you need to focus on. Be honest with yourself, could you realistically achieve some of those goals before the original deadline you set? I bet you probably can. You need to be strict with yourself and set both short-term and long-term goals.

It's time to **take action**! They say good things come to those who wait, well I believe good things come to those who go out there and grab them with both hands. You are reading this book for a reason and it isn't to pick up another self-help book the minute you see the back of this one. In the words of Henry Ford, "If you always do what you've always done, then you'll always get what you've always got." If you want something in your life to change, you have to do something differently. At the beginning of this book I told you that statistically only 8% of people reach their goals. Do you want to be in the 92% who feel like they never seem to get there, or the 8% who get what they want? That's what I thought. It's time to stop wishing and start taking action.

Let's expand further on the fear of change, it's called metathesiophobia and is something that affects us all regardless of our behaviour, but in my experience it's more prevalent within those who have a high level of Green behaviour. I want you to know that these feelings are perfectly normal and something we all experience at some point throughout our lives. The Greens' drive for a stable environment contradicts and outweighs any desire for change, even when they know it's a change for the better.

The fear of change is a massive hurdle for the Greens, it's not that they don't strive for more, it's just the thought of change can be a crippling fear. Not only does the need for stability cause them to resist change but it also means they can take a little longer to adapt than others. COVID-19 not only forced change on people but it came with no warning. The Greens had no time to process the change, heightening all of their fixed traits, leaving them with a concoction of anxiety, fear and uncertainty.

The fear of change is a deviant monster that uses the power of the fixed mindset to get its own way. When you're thinking about your goal and what could happen if you actually achieve it, it's more than likely that the metathesiophobia forces you to jump straight towards the negatives. Think about the worst things that can happen, it will usually sound like this: 'What if I fail? What if people laugh at me? What if I am not good enough? What if I don't like it?' I'm sure you've experienced one if not all of these thoughts at some point. These are coming from the fixed mindset's natural instinct to protect you and stop you from hurting yourself. The fixed mindset doesn't understand that not all changes are bad. When metathesiophobia sets in, reprogramme your thought process using the SMASH IT! method to overcome a fixed mindset and take growth actions.

The part that I really want you to focus on is step 4, the benefits. Stop thinking about the potential negative outcomes and start acknowledging the positives. Stop thinking about the worst-case scenario and start imagining the best-case scenario. When you get to this point I want you to write a physical list of pros and cons of achieving your goals. Usually when my clients do this they realise that a lot of the negative thoughts they were having were irrational and the pros far outweigh the cons. Imagine your goal is to earn a promotion at work, your list might look a little like this:

Pros	Cons
Pay rise	Potentially more hours
Flexible hours could make meeting up with my friends after work easier	If I work late, I might miss the Wednesday pub quiz with my friends
Get to spend more time away from the desk	Have to drive further to external meetings
I could be great at the job	I might hate the job
This could lead to further promotions in the future	More travel means earlier starts
All travel and expenses are paid for by the company	

Another big obstacle for the Greens is self-belief. They lack confidence and doubt their decisions which is why they often rely on their partners or friends to help guide them. The only problem with this is that when everyone else is making your decisions you end up doing what they want and not what you want. When a Green does take the wheel and decide for themselves, they are so scared of getting it wrong it can take so long for them to make up their mind that sometimes they miss out on the opportunity.

Imagine you're a big fan of the band No Doubt fronted by Gwen Stefani. You're out having dinner with your friends and Gwen walks in. You can't believe your luck, you've been a fan for years. Everyone in the restaurant is crowding around her and asking for autographs. You're thinking about what you're going to say to her when it's your turn, but what if Gwen doesn't want to talk to you? She has already been bombarded by everyone else asking for autographs and selfies. Perhaps you should just leave her to have her dinner in peace. You can't imagine what it must be like to have strangers invading your personal space all the time, poor Gwen she is just a human like everyone else.

But then again, she is one of your favourite singers of all time, and why shouldn't you get to meet her like all the others in the restaurant? Perhaps you could just tell her you're a big fan and leave it at that, but she probably hears that all the time, if you're going to disturb her dinner shouldn't you at least make it worth her while and not waste her time? You wouldn't want her to think you're a time waster, or even worse a pathetic loser who obsesses over her all the time.

Meanwhile, whilst you were debating on the best course of action, your Red friend chatted with Gwen about how she rocks 'Don't Speak' on Karaoke and got an epic photo, and your Yellow friend has wangled free tickets and backstage passes to her gig tonight. You didn't even get the opportunity to say anything to Gwen because by the time you've made up your mind she has left the building. What the hell just happened? You can't believe that you missed that once in a lifetime opportunity, you're so mad at yourself for letting the fear hold you back again.

From No Doubt to self-doubt, this holds you back, not just when Gwen is in the building but in your everyday life. You are scared that you won't be good enough, so much so that sometimes you don't even see the point in trying. I am going to talk about confidence in more detail later but here are a few things that can help you specifically as a high Green. 'I think I am, therefore I am' – I have no idea who said this or where I heard it, but it's something that has stuck with me. I said this a lot to myself when I first started my business. It's my way of reminding myself that I can be whatever I want and that the only person with any power to stop me is me.

Positive affirmations are a great way to start building self-confidence and self-belief. A positive affirmation can be anything you want. You can keep it brief or get detailed, the purpose is to inspire you, give you that buzz of confidence that makes you feel like you can do anything. Affirmations can work for anyone. The most important thing is that they are personal to you. Give it a go now, write down three positive affirmations. Then look at yourself in the mirror and say them. This may feel strange at first but the more you do it, the easier it will become.

The reason I ask you to look in the mirror is because I want you to make the connection between the words coming out of your mouth and the person staring back at you. My goal for you is to get to a place where you can stand confidently in front of a mirror and really believe the affirmations you are telling yourself. Practise your affirmations as often as you can.

My second piece of advice for you is to build a strong support circle. As a relationship-based introvert, you enjoy spending time with those you hold close to your heart, and you care what they think. You need to fill your life with people who support and motivate you, people who lift you up, not knock you down. Like a river flowing into the sea, it's easy to choose the path of least resistance. This also happens when we choose our support network. We have the tendency to surround ourselves with the people like us, the yes-men who agree with everything we say.

The secret to growth is to be open to feedback and take it as a mechanism to aid development. This means surrounding yourself with all the colours and not just those who are the same as you. This can be difficult at times. It may seem that comments from your Red friends are like snippets from the film *Mean Girls*, but we know that being tactful is not always natural to them, so don't discard their opinions as more often than not, they are coming from a place of concern even if at first it doesn't seem like that. It may just be the push in the back you need to get you going.

Finally, my last tip for you high Greens is to stop seeking validation. One of the biggest pitfalls for a Green is the lack of trust they have towards making their own decisions, again this is down to a lack of self-belief. Instead, they rely on those around them to make their decisions, often saying, "What do you think I should do?" and "Do you think it's OK if I do this?" Now don't get me wrong, it is absolutely OK to ask for a bit of advice but asking for someone's opinion isn't the same as letting them make your decisions. I see this a lot in Greens. It's easy to get to a point where you don't even realise you're doing it and, before you know it, you can't even remember what you like watching on TV because you always let your partner decide. The thing is, when you rely on someone else to make all your decisions, you are never going to get what you want, you will get what they want for you and that isn't the same.

The positive affirmations and having a strong support circle will already be a step forward in taking back control of your life, you need to learn to trust yourself again. One of the best ways to do this is by scheduling some 'me time', try to set aside some time each week where you can be alone and do whatever you want. You might struggle at first to decide what to do or even feel a little lonely. Perhaps you will even feel guilty for being selfish with your time, but it will help you become more independent and learn to trust yourself in the long run. You might even feel empowered after doing this.

Allowing yourself to have your own time means you can deposit in *your* Bank of Give Back and Faffing Around. Coming back to Alison

Edgar's Big Balls, a lot of the time you place your own needs as a Ping-Pong Ball, making other people's needs your Basketballs. It's time to stop forgoing your needs for other people and take back control.

There are a lot of tips and advice here that you can start implementing today. Let's go over the main points before moving on:

1. Take action - Stop procrastinating. Start doing things today and stop putting them off until tomorrow. Think carefully about the time constraints you put on your goals and don't be afraid to hit the ground running.
2. Embrace change - Remember that change is a part of life and more often than not it is a change for the better. Focus on the positives and rationalise the negatives.
3. Believe in yourself and focus on YOU - You can do anything you put your mind to, the only person that is stopping you from moving forward is YOU. Have confidence and trust in yourself to do what is best for you. Deposit regularly in your Banks of Balance, and manage your balls effectively, it's time to focus on YOU!

The Blues

Compliance is key for someone with a high Blue behaviour. As task-focused introverts, they respect the rules and appreciate law and order are needed to create a well-structured environment which runs smoothly. Structure is the key word here, Blues love structure and don't cope so well with spontaneity and risk-taking.

Being task-focused, the Blues, much like Reds, like to be acknowledged for their work. However, where they differ is the results: Reds get things done to be the first but when a Blue does something they want to do it right. They want everything they do to be the best it can and always seek perfection. They are their own worst critics, always striving to do better and achieve more.

The introverted part of Blues means they are quiet and independent, they are more than happy to do things on their own, not relying on anyone else. Someone who is Blue will be very specific about who they choose to spend their time with. Even though they are introverted, if they find themselves in an argument they have no shame in fighting to the death using facts and figures to back up their points and authority.

Deep thinkers, the Blues don't make decisions lightly. They are very careful and ensure they take all the factors into consideration before making any decisions. They often rely upon facts and proven evidence to help them and you can be sure they will be thorough in conducting research to aid the decision-making process. Not only does this way of thinking reduce risk, it means someone who is Blue can sometimes come across as self-righteous, confident that they are always right.

Usually, when I talk about Blue behaviour, the person that comes to most people's minds is Sheldon from the popular TV show *The Big Bang Theory*. But Sheldon isn't real and is based on stereotypical behaviour types. Similar to the Greens, you don't often see high Blues in the spotlight, where you will find them is usually heading up the tech industry.

Mark Zuckerberg, founder of Facebook, is someone who exhibits high Blue behaviour. He is one of the most recognisable CEOs in the world and for good reason: his spotlight came as a result of his work yet he still maintains a private life, using his status to address work-related projects and charity work. The fact that he has already achieved so much and is worth an incredible amount of money doesn't stop him from inventing and developing new things, he is always striving to achieve more.

As much as they would like to believe it, the Blues are not perfect. They have their fixed and growth traits like everyone else. On the bad days they are hung up on their own ideals of what is perfect and refuse to accept anyone's help. But on the good days they can understand that there will always be room for improvement and are able to be objective when making decisions. Here's a clearer look at the fixed and growth traits of someone with high Blue behaviour.

Fixed Traits	Growth Traits
Fear of failure	Determined
Perfectionist	Strives for improvement
Risk averse	Reliable
Self-righteous	Self-assured
Loner	Independent
Results-driven	Ambitious

What about you, are you a high Blue? Do the same as before and read through the following statements, mark down which ones you agree with. If you agree with the statements, then it is more than likely that you are a high Blue.

- I appreciate something more when there is a clear set of guidelines to follow
- I appreciate that a good job takes time
- I appreciate it when people do not disturb my concentration, especially when I am at work
- I appreciate it when things are done accurately and on time
- I appreciate it when the information I am provided with is based on reliable data

- I am irritated when I am forced to make quick decisions without considering all of the facts
- I am irritated when people don't follow the rules
- I am irritated when others try to encourage me to break the rules
- I am irritated when people display tactile and over-affectionate behaviour
- I am irritated when someone invades my personal space

No one appreciates the smaller things in life quite like the Blues. Their task-focused minds make them a sucker for detail, they always want to ensure everything is just as it should be. Attention to detail is a great quality to have, and that's coming from a woman who doesn't have a detail-orientated bone in her body! However, it can also be one of the biggest setbacks for a Blue when it comes to getting what they want.

My husband Neil is bright blue! Neil and I got married in Jamaica, just the two of us. We had planned on returning home to a big reception to celebrate with all of our friends and family. It was set to be one hell of a party – trust me, nobody loves a wedding as much as the Scottish! Neil knew that he would have to make a speech at the reception to thank all of our loved ones for supporting us and coming together to celebrate. Being a Blue, Neil couldn't just wing the speech when we arrived, oh no, he had to plan out what he was going to say. Public speaking had never been Neil's thing, he wanted to make sure that his wedding speech was word perfect, he didn't want to miss anyone out or forget any of the important details.

The two weeks we spent in Jamaica after our wedding was supposed to be our honeymoon. I spent my days basking in the sun and sipping on pina coladas, enjoying what felt like our very own slice of paradise. Neil on the other hand spent the two weeks fussing over his speech, writing and rewriting until it was word perfect. He would practise and practise day in and day out, to be quite frank I think even the hotel staff got sick of hearing him practise by the time we left.

On the day we were due to fly home our plane was delayed (you'll know all about this if you have read *Secrets of Successful Sales*) and by the time we made our grand entrance at our wedding reception, in true Scottish style our guests had got the party started without us and were well on their way to a good time. When it came to the time for Neil's speech everyone just wanted to keep the party going, so I took the microphone, thanked everyone for coming and made a toast to wrap it up. Neil didn't even make the speech he had been stressing about for the last two weeks, but we did have a great night celebrating.

The purpose of this story is to show you that as a Blue, being a perfectionist can actually be the thing that holds you back. In this instance, Neil didn't get to make his speech because a spotlight-loving Yellow (me) jumped in there first. I have spent enough time with Blues to know that even if Neil had made his speech as planned, he still wouldn't have been satisfied. One because in his eyes it was never perfect, he would always be able to pick a hole in it somewhere, and two because his captive audience were less captive and more sloshed.

There is no doubt about it that a Blue will always strive to achieve their best, and of course it is great that they are open to change and willing to make improvements. However, there comes a point when you have to accept that not everything can be perfect and that's OK. The Blues get so caught up in always trying to achieve perfection that they never actually get to cross the goal off their list and get what they want.

As a Blue, I know that the moment you set your goal you will follow it with a detailed criteria of what achievement means, as a Blue you are great at being Specific. I want you to limit your criteria to 5-10 points and once you've set it leave it alone. As a rule follower, one of the reasons for this is because they fear failure. Blues, like the Reds, want to be the best at everything they do. Unlike the Reds they actually care about the results.

You shouldn't be afraid of failing; as the old adage goes, 'It's better to have tried and failed than to never have tried at all'. Do you think Torville and Dean nailed the *Bolero* first time round? Did they heck! They had to fall and crack themselves on the ice a few times before they could take home the gold medal. Every time you fall, you learn. Like the five-year-old on the ice skating rink, you have to fall down a few times and scrape a few knees to learn. Being afraid to fail is like being afraid to learn, it doesn't make sense.

I am the first to admit that there is always room for improvement. But the Blues take this to another level, always picking holes and looking for mistakes, settling for nothing less than perfection. The thing is if you're always looking for the negatives it can be hard to see how great something already is. I want you to focus on moving away from the results-driven way of the fixed mindset and towards the effort-driven approach of the growth mindset. Life goals aren't like school exams, no one is grading you, the only person that can say if you pass or fail is yourself. If you have done your best, you physically cannot do any more than that, recognise that putting in 100% effort is as big an achievement as getting an A grade on a maths test.

When you focus on effort the results will come; only focus on results and you'll be forever chasing a version of perfection that doesn't exist. Blues tend to love guidelines, which means they can overdo it when setting goal criteria and what starts out as a few points can end up being the Magna Carta. Try to keep your criteria short and sweet. I know that SMART says to be specific but also remember the other aspects. Don't set a goal so specific that it is impossible.

In an attempt to achieve perfection, it is easy to lose sight of why you wanted something in the first place. This is often the case for someone who is a high Blue. The results become more important than their WHY. Your WHY should be your biggest motivator, not the result. Remind yourself of your WHY on a regular basis to ensure your focus is in the right place, whether this means creating a vision board or writing it down and reading it. Don't lose sight of your WHY in a bid for perfection.

I just want to take a minute to recognise that in an Instagram world the desire for perfection is something that is growing within all the behaviour types. We all see things on the internet, and we build up ideas and expectations in our heads of what perfection looks like. The key thing to recognise here is that we all have our own idea of what perfection means, so stop doing things because you think others will like it. Do it because you like it. Do it because it's what YOU want.

To sum it up, my advice for ensuring you, someone with high Blue behaviour, gets what you want is:

1. Effort over results - Focus on always doing your best and knowing that you can't do any more than that. Giving something 100% effort is an achievement in itself.
2. Make it SMART, not impossible - Follow the SMART system when you write your goals but remember being specific doesn't mean being perfect.
3. Remember WHY - Don't lose sight of why you set your goal in the first place.

Colours at Conflict

As you already know, you are a mix of all four of the behaviour types, but usually have one or two that are more dominant. Based on what you've already learned I am hoping that you have got a bit of a grasp on what your dominant colours might be. The different behaviours work together in different ways; some complement each other, whereas others can cause internal conflict. It is common to have two dominant colours that contradict each other, which can result in further hurdles when trying to hit your goals.

There are three behaviour combinations that I am going to discuss, these are considered to be the ones that cause a higher level of internal conflict. The colours that struggle to work together are the ones that are positioned diagonally opposite each other on the graph below. This means the Red/Green and Yellow/Blue combinations. The final concoction of colours I would like to talk about is the mixed behaviour; this is when someone doesn't have one or two dominant behaviours and instead has a fairly even spread, this is more uncommon but does happen.

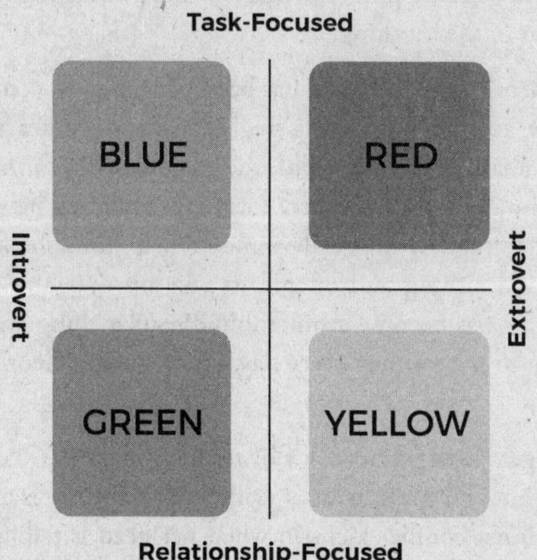

Red/Greens

Let's start with the Red/Greens, this is the combination I see the most out of the three we are going to discuss. In the top right of the graph, we have the task-focused extroverts, the Reds. Directly opposite from them in the bottom left we have the Greens, the relationship-focused introverts.

When two polar opposite colours have to work together like this, it usually becomes a battle of the head and heart. The head operates under task-focused behaviours and the heart is ruled by those with a relationship focus.

Let me introduce you to Georgia, she struggles regularly with her inner conflict. Georgia lives in a small village with her partner and two children. She starts work at 9am and has to drop her kids off to school before she goes in. She works in the next town and traffic can often be gridlocked at rush hour. Between making breakfast, convincing the kids to put on their shoes and putting on the laundry, time is tight in the morning.

Recently Georgia's friend Liam has been struggling to manage to get his daughter to school. Liam is a single dad and his mum is currently unwell. As Liam is an only child, the responsibility for his mum is down to him. Georgia feels sorry for him, she knows how hard it is to be in this situation and really wants to help him. She noticed his struggle one morning and offered to take his daughter to school. Since then, it has become a much more regular thing and adds 10 minutes on to the journey every day, often making Georgia late for work.

As a manager, Georgia has a lot of responsibility. Between looking after her team and projects, it is really important she is at work on time. The inner conflict kicks in when her head is telling her 'you must be at work at 9' but her heart is telling her she needs to help out her friend. She thinks she can't be a good role model for her team if she is turning up late for work and is worried the standards may start to slip. She now has to make a decision to let Liam down or suffer the consequences at work.

The fight between your Red head and Green heart sends you into overdrive and you start to panic, going into overwhelm. When this happens there is no winning; whether you decide to go ahead and take control or not, as a Red/Green it will be a lose-lose situation. If Georgia was a pure high Red, she would take control, tell Liam she can no longer take his daughter to school, and not think another minute about it. However, when there is a high level of Green in the mix this isn't possible. The Greens can be very retrospective and, as you know, are full of self-doubt.

Whatever decision she decides to make in the end, she will always look back and be thinking 'what if?' 'What if Liam thinks I'm a bad person?' 'What if he can't get his daughter to school any other way?' 'What if he goes out and his mum has a fall?' You will always be looking back wondering if you did the right thing.

As a result of this way of thinking you become afraid to commit to any decisions in your own personal life because what if it's wrong? The Red in you is stubborn and reinforces this way of thinking, making the resistance to change even stronger than if you were just a pure Green.

Yellow/Blues

The Yellows, bottom right, are the relationship-focused extroverts, whereas the Blues, top left, are at the opposite ends of the scales as the task-focused introverts. Whilst the Yellows are seen as the irrational, spontaneous types, making decisions off the cuff, the Blues have always respected the rules and found comfort in facts and routine. Again, when the two come together it becomes a battle of the head and heart. The Yellow in you wants to get up and dance on the tables while singing your heart out to Scouting for Girls' hit single, *She's So Lovely* (a personal favourite of mine). But the Blue in you is mentally performing a risk assessment, keeping your feet firmly on the ground, before realistically questioning how good an idea it is to get up on a rickety old table and start throwing shapes.

More often than not those who have a high Yellow in them will have a thirst for the spotlight, always aware of their impact on the room, it's a dominant trait. When you pair Yellow and Blue behaviour together you get someone who is socially aware, able to pick up on the tiniest changes in their environment that would go unnoticed by most, this is thanks to the detail-oriented Blue mind.

This hypersensitivity to their social surroundings can be great but it's also where a lot of inner conflict starts. A Yellow/Blue will read into minor details, overthinking and analysing someone's opinion, searching for criticism and rejection when it isn't even there. Whilst a Yellow is someone who is usually confident, the battle between the head and heart means a Yellow/Blue can at times be full of self-doubt. The conflicting messages stemming from a mixed Yellow and Blue behaviour results in someone who is always second guessing themselves, looking for hidden messages in everything they see, effectively setting themselves up for what they perceive to be failure before they have even begun.

Mixed Behaviour

This is a combination that is quite rare, but it does happen and is therefore worth discussing. We are all a combination of the four colours, I've already said it multiple times, but I really want to hammer this one home. Every single one of us is a blend of Red, Yellow, Green and Blue. The difference here is that someone with what I call a Mixed behaviour doesn't have a dominant behaviour, instead each of the four colours are fairly evenly spread.

What does this mean? Well as you can imagine, a lack of one or two dominating behaviours is the ultimate conflict. Think of it like driving a car. It's as though four pals have jumped in a car ready for the ultimate road trip, but for some reason they have all jumped in the passenger seat and just come along for the ride. With no one behind the wheel the car isn't going anywhere. They all want to put their ten pennies worth in, wanting to go here, there and everywhere, but with no real driver they can't even back the car off the driveway.

In all the examples I have given around internal conflict the dominant colours work against each other, resulting in a reinforcement of fixed traits. But it doesn't have to be this way. If you have more than one dominant behaviour, it means you have twice as many strengths at your disposal. And if you're lacking a dominant colour, it means you have such a wide range to your behaviour that the potential is immeasurable. You are more aware now of your behaviour type and what it means than ever before. You know the strengths and weaknesses of each behaviour. Try to identify which of these is more prevalent with you and use them. Harness the growth traits from the different parts of your behaviour and find ways for them to cooperate and work together to overcome the conflict and create positive actions.

Every behaviour approach has its strengths and weaknesses, none are perfect but they are all amazing in their own way. The more you embrace your behaviour and use it to your advantage, the easier it will become to get what you want. In the words of Cyndi Lauper's hit 80s song: "Don't be afraid to let them show your true colours, your true colours are beautiful like a rainbow."

CASE STUDY: MEET CHRIS...

The Situation

Chris is a single mother in her 40s to 'one wonderful daughter and an adorable dog'. She is a business founder, providing training and project management services to organisations. That's her day job, but by night she is an entertainer, she loves to bring joy to the masses through her acting and singing. Chris's ultimate goal is to get her business to a place where she can reduce her hours and spend more time travelling with her daughter and up on the stage doing what she loves.

The Problem

Since starting her business Chris has wanted to complete her PRINCE 2 project management qualification as she knows this could help secure more clients and ultimately grow the business. It would be another step closer to achieving her big goal.

In the new year, Chris signed up to study an online course to finally get the qualification she has been putting off since starting her business several years ago. She had decided that this year was dedicated to developing her skills, this would be the year she would finally get the qualification.

To make sure she completed the course, Chris put together a study plan, dedicating specific time to learning, organising her folders and resources and even turning part of her office into a study corner. Four months later and Chris was no further forward than she was at the beginning of the year, her study plan was great, but she was struggling to follow it. There was always something more fun to do, "I couldn't shut out the distraction from other people." Not only was Chris angry and frustrated with herself for once again letting life distract her from getting what she really wants, but she was also going to have to pay an extra fee to extend the course, which only added to the feelings of self-loathing.

This was a feeling Chris had become all too familiar with, she often found herself caught in this internal struggle, half of her wanting to do the sensible thing and the other half of her grabbing at every opportunity thrown at her, ensuring she didn't miss out. She always felt like she was torn, never quite managing to find the balance. It didn't matter what she did she always felt guilty about not doing something, she couldn't win.

The Win-Win

Chris signed up to my four-part webinar series during the first COVID-19 lockdown. We had known each other for a while, Chris having previously attended a workshop and saw a post for the webinars just as she was going through the vicious cycle of self-loathing that she had been through so many times before.

"I was relieved," said Chris after attending the webinar. She learned about the behaviours and identified that she exhibited Yellow/Blue behaviour. As you know by now, Blue and Yellow are complete opposites. She was great at planning and organising but when it came down to actually studying, she was always distracted by the 'bing' of her phone notifications or getting drawn into conversation with her daughter and clients.

"I finally understood why I hadn't been successful at my plan and stopped beating myself up over not doing it and decided that now I understood why I was being distracted, I could put a new plan in place."

Now that Chris understood why she did what she did, she realised she had to stop being so hard on herself and instead of fighting against herself had to find a way to work with all elements of her behaviour. She came up with a new study plan, this time taking into account her Blue/Yellow tendencies, that's where the win-win is. She scheduled shorter study sessions and built in breaks specifically for checking social media and emails; this would decrease her chances of getting distracted and satisfy her Yellow needs to do something fun and make sure she wasn't missing out on anything. Not only that but she moved her study corner to a quieter area where she could be alone and turned off all phone notifications to ensure there would be no more 'bings'.

One of the things that Chris took away from the session was the way I described a Blue/Yellow: "The Yellow will want to dance on the table, but the Blue will have to do a risk assessment first." She now has the quote written on her whiteboard to remind her of who she is and to not be so hard on herself.

The Techniques

The most important thing that Chris did was identifying her behaviour; understanding why she acted and reacted to situations in a particular way helped her to accept who she was. She was constantly fighting and arguing with herself before the webinar but learning about the behaviours helped put things into perspective. Through understanding the colours, Chris learned about the strengths and weaknesses of each behaviour, identifying measures she could put in place to satisfy both the Blue and Yellow in her.

To change your behaviour, you must first understand it. Often those who face internal conflict like Chris will try to change the way they do things without ever understanding why they did them in the first place. When you know why you behave in a particular way it is a lot easier to manage it and use it to your advantage.

Driving Forces

By now as a result of completing the magazine quiz and learning more about the DISC model, you will be starting to develop a deeper level of self-awareness. You will have more knowledge as to why at times you have reacted the way you have in different situations, affecting you getting what YOU want. Whilst this gives you a good baseline to where you roughly sit, there are definitely more robust systems out there, like Clarity4D and Ensize, which provide more accurate reports.

Each tool has its advantages, but there were two things that drew me to Ensize. First was the simple way in which it explained the model and the results. The second thing was the emphasis it places on the values and driving forces we each have as humans. The Ensize analysis identifies how our values make up who we are, and from this we develop driving forces throughout our lives, which help us make decisions and choose which paths to take. These then impact our behaviour and how we perceive our environment.

Driving forces and values are the key distinguishing factors between different people. Two people may have the exact same behaviours, but because of the difference in their driving forces they do things differently. For example, Donald Trump and Michael Jordan are both Red behaviour types. I don't want to get political, but whilst one is donating $50m to activist projects, the other has been banned from social media for his questionable views.

Before moving on, I want to talk more about driving forces. I want to explain what I mean when I refer to them and how they impact your behaviour, and ultimately inspire what YOU want.

What are driving forces? These are your motivators or attitudes that derive as a result of your values and personal beliefs. In 1928, philosopher Dr Eduard Spranger published his theory 'Types of Men'. He theorised that humans' actions resulted from their attitudes, which he believed could be divided into six categories. Ensize have expanded on this theory, renaming the categories and breaking one of the groups up, creating seven key driving forces (Ensize, 2019b):

1. **Economic** - A focus on money and what is profitable, providing the most financial return for their investment. A person's investment in something can be both time and money. People who have a strong economical drive strive for the security that comes with money and financial assets.
2. **Ethical and Moral** - Someone with a strong ethical and moral driving force tends to have a comprehensive set of values for what they perceive to be right and wrong, which they use to guide them. They will focus on what is fair and support what they believe to be the 'forces of good'.
3. **Knowledge** - Learning and discovering is key for someone who has knowledge as a dominant driving force. They will search for the facts and seek to understand the context of something, often looking at the world from a critical but rational perspective.
4. **Power and Influence** - Someone with this as a strong driving force seeks control and power. This can mean self-control, authority over others as well as control over decisions and how things are carried out.

5. **Consideration** - Other people are the main focus, individuals who have a strong drive for consideration will often sacrifice what they want if it could have a negative impact on another human being.

6. **Practical** - Likes to show others what they have made. They tend to be skilful and have the ability to start, manage and complete projects. They value craft and the sensible use of resources and manufacturing.

7. **Self-fulfilment** - Have a strong interest in personal development and wellbeing. They value an environment which allows for creativity, innovation and expression of their own and other's ideas.

Spranger (1928) believed that out of these different attitude categories, we all have two that are stronger and influence the remaining four in varying degrees. A person's behaviour is then driven by their two strongest driving forces. One of the key points that I want you to take from this is how the driving forces impact your behaviour. Everyone's behaviour is a combination of the four colours which makes us all slightly different; when you add the driving forces to this, it separates us even further as individuals. This is why if you lined up four high Greens, they would still all be different because the driving forces behind their Green behaviour would not be the same.

Let's imagine you don't recycle a plastic bottle. Someone with a strong ethical and moral driving force could feel very upset by this and angry, they would then act accordingly. However, someone who is high Green but has strong economic driving forces might be nonplussed about not recycling the plastic bottle. Both are high Greens, but their driving forces are different and therefore would exhibit different aspects of Green behaviour when reacting to the incident.

The driving forces reflect the different kinds of goals we set for ourselves. If you look at your WHY I am sure you will be able to identify which driving force your WHY represents. Have a go at it now and see what you come up with. In the left column write down your goal. In the right column write down which driving force your goal corresponds to. This might help you identify what motivates you.

This should take you 5-10 minutes to complete

Your Goal	**Driving Force**

Driving forces can help explain why some goals are easier or harder to hit than others, this feeds back to your WHY. Without realising, your reason WHY will mirror your driving forces.

I am going to tell you a story about two of my friends, Sarah and Michelle. Sarah and Michelle work for the same organisation but in two different branches. The two friends are talking about how a more senior role has become available in Sarah's office and Michelle really thinks Sarah should go for it. Sarah isn't sure about taking the senior role, Michelle has already been promoted twice in the last 18 months. Climbing the ladder has been so easy for Michelle, she doesn't understand why Sarah keeps passing up opportunities for progression. This is where the driving forces come into play. You see, Michelle's driving forces are power and influence and economical gain. For her, a promotion is a no brainer, more authority and more money, how can she lose?

Sarah on the other hand is driven by self-fulfilment and consideration for those in her life. A promotion needs to be more than just about money for her. When Sarah thinks about taking a step up the career ladder, she thinks how it will impact her work-life balance and her relationships with her co-workers. She will be thinking about her colleague, Freddie, who has been in the company longer than her, how will he feel if Sarah gets a promotion before him? Where Michelle will simply jump at the opportunity to earn a pay rise, for Sarah this isn't the most important factor.

This doesn't necessarily mean that Sarah doesn't want a promotion as much as Michelle does, it just means she has different requirements to meet. When you understand this, things become a lot easier. Especially when you pair what you know about your driving forces with what you know about WHY you want something. See, if Sarah knew all this about herself she could negotiate a deal that works for both her and her organisation to create a win-win situation. If Sarah's employer knew this then even better, they would know how to motivate her and approach the idea of a promotion in a different way, but we will discuss more about that in the next section.

Like Maslow's, driving forces are fluid and can change throughout your life based on your circumstances. For example, if economic was your biggest driving force and you won the lottery, your driving force may move to consideration as financial security would no longer be your top priority. Alternatively, if you were in a stable relationship where your partner was the main breadwinner and you split up, economic could become a priority.

The driving forces are very closely tied with Maslow's Hierarchy of Needs to create your WHY. When you bring your knowledge of the two together, it helps to build a clearer image and explains the motivation behind the goals you set for yourself. Each one of the driving forces can be present at all levels of Maslow's hierarchy. Both your position in the hierarchy and dominant driving forces can impact each other.

The Vicious Circle

I can't stop crying! They're not the kind of tears which elegantly roll down your face like you see in films when the Hollywood starlet watches her long-lost lover from afar. No, they are like heavy raindrops that flood my face as I wail loudly out of control, the type of crying you hear at a funeral as someone buries their nearest and dearest and feels like their heart has been ripped right out of their chest. But I'm not at a funeral so why am I crying? Why can't I stop the horrific sobs that keep forcing their way out my mouth? I'm a rational and sensible adult, so why am I making this uncontrollable noise?

I look around, I'm all alone. Well not completely alone, I'm void of adult company, my two babies are here, they are two years and 16 months old. All they do is cry, screaming and wailing at me all the time, they can't speak but I know they need me. I want to hold them, to soothe them, but I can't because I don't know who is crying louder, me or them. It's like a competition to see who can make the most noise, all three of us bawling our eyes out, the louder I get, the louder they get, and the more they cry, the harder I cry.

My whole life I've been completely in control, I can do anything. Hell, I travelled the world for six years with nothing but myself and my backpack. Surely, if I can do that I can do this. But I can't. I can't do this. I try, every time I sort out one crying baby the other one starts, but I don't know what they want, I don't know how to help them. Not only that but my incontinent dog is weeing and pooing all over the place. I just want it to stop! When will it all stop? Eventually when it does stop, I start crying and that sets them off again. It's like I'm stuck in a revolving door to hell, I want to get off, I so desperately want to get off but there is no way out. I feel completely and utterly helpless.

I have no one to turn to, everyone thinks I'm OK because let's face it, I always am. I'm the leader of the pack, the one who pulls the world together, the one who organises everyone else's lives. I'm the shepherd in a world of sheep. But I'm **not** OK! Given the chance I would leave this earth in the blink of an eye, I'm a shit mum and everything around me is crumbling. Everyone would be better off without me. I am useless! I have no worth! I am nothing!

This was the story which was repeated in my head as often as Tinky Winky spoke to La La and Dipsy on the *Teletubbies*. And these were the words that flew round and round in my head every minute of every day. My life was a mess!

Every day I did my best to make sure it was different from the day before, but it never was. If I wasn't crying, my babies were, and if they were, then I was definitely crying louder. I tried to unpick what the hell was happening. When did my life turn upside down? How was it possible that I could go from being more or less a superwoman – sales hero, wife, daughter, sister and friend of the year – to this? A blubbering mess with no means of escape. It was like I was having an out of body experience. It felt like someone else had taken over my body and I was sitting on the sidelines, watching as they lived my life. Looking back, it's hard to describe my feelings, apart from out and out despair, it was like I was numb, I felt everything and nothing at the same time.

I didn't know how long this had been going on for; being up all night trying to feed a baby and soothing a teething toddler, all the days had started to roll into one never-ending hell. My only solace came from the weekly catch-ups with my friends. We would go round each other's houses and have actual adult conversations about things other than how little Johnny could read a book and run a marathon before the age of one. Mothers can be extremely competitive but luckily none of my friends were like this. It was at one of these weekly meetups that my friend Becky – always the thoughtful, caring one – had realised that I needed professional help. I can vividly remember the day she called the doctor.

I had always managed to hide my pain and suffering under the happy, smiley clown face. I would wear my happy-go-lucky attitude as if it were battle armour. However, on that dull and drab September afternoon the facade slipped, I could not pretend anymore. I finally admitted to my friends how I was feeling and told them I couldn't carry on.

Prior to this experience, suicidal thoughts had been a fleeting glimpse in my life, but during this time they sat at the forefront of my mind. I thought my kids would be better off without me. It felt good to finally say all my thoughts and feelings out loud. Becky wasn't shocked when I shared all of this with her, she didn't judge or try to reason with me. Instead, she calmly called the doctor, informed them I was suffering from postnatal depression and demanded an appointment **now**!

When the doctor diagnosed me, I was both relieved and shocked. Relieved that I wasn't going mad, but actually had a hormonal imbalance which was clouding my judgment and explained why I had been feeling the way I had. Shocked that I had actually shared my anxiety and fears with someone rather than trying to keep them locked away in my head. Postnatal depression is not uncommon and if you had put a Ladbrokes bet on me having it, I would have said the odds would have been slim to none. Depression and mental health can affect anyone, even those that think they are invincible.

I share a lot of personal stories through my work, but never this one. So why am I sharing it now? Is it to shine a light on mental health? Sure I think that is important but that is not my intention. I am sharing it because I want to show you that it doesn't matter where you start, it's about where you finish.

It wasn't easy to bounce back after my diagnosis of postnatal depression, the doctor didn't click his fingers and magic me better overnight. I followed the process of cognitive behavioural therapy (CBT).

In case you don't know, CBT is a talking therapy that can help overcome issues by altering the way you behave. It is based on the concept that your thoughts create feelings, your feelings create behaviours, and the behaviours reinforce thoughts. It suggests that if a situation is not necessarily a positive one, you may, because of these factors, be stuck in a vicious circle.

This was my experience while I was going through postnatal depression. Every time my babies cried and I struggled to settle them, I felt like a hopeless mother. These thoughts of hopelessness and failure circulated my mind, and my behaviour became a reflection of this. No, I didn't ignore my kids, but I was overwhelmed, daily tasks seemed near impossible to deal with. I could barely meet my physiological needs like eating, sleeping and showering. I stopped cleaning the house, the carpet was a sea of toys. In my head I knew that I should be getting outside, getting fresh air, that's what they always tell you to do when you're feeling down. But I couldn't, the idea of having to leave the house with the two boys filled me with anxiety, what if Connor started crying or Kieran threw a tantrum? What if I couldn't calm them down and everyone would see I was a bad mother? This only reinforced the thought that everyone would be better off without me.

Dr Aaron T Beck in the 1960s developed CBT as a way to break the pattern (Beck Institute, 2020). The idea is to isolate the three components –thoughts, feelings and behaviours – and treat them all as individual aspects. Research shows that by doing this you can flip a switch on the negative cycle and improve the overall way you feel about the situation. CBT helped me through my depression and whilst it is often used to battle mental health, it is something that I think can be used in all aspects of life.

I am going to show you how following the CBT method will help you get what YOU want. I am not a qualified therapist by any means, what I will share with you is very low touch. If you are struggling with your mental health as you read this, please, please tell a loved one, confide in a friend and seek professional help. You are not alone.

Let's use the hypothetical example of Ashley to explore this further. Ashley has just had his 17th birthday; all his friends have already started their driving lessons and he wants to as well. If he could drive, his parents would let him stay out later and he wouldn't have to get on the stinking bus to college every day. As his first driving lesson approaches, Ashley starts thinking to himself what if I make a mistake? What if something goes wrong and I crash? This starts as a fleeting thought but as he climbs into the driver's seat for the first time, it's all he thinks about. This thought makes him feel anxious, he's nervous as it is but now he feels sick to his stomach, overcome with the fear that he could cause an accident.

He grips the steering wheel so tight his knuckles turn white; he's sweating profusely and the only sound he can hear is his heart pounding against his chest. He tries to listen to the instructor but he's too distracted, he slowly follows his step-by-step instructions trying to pull away, when he stalls the car. He tries again and this time is successful, he drives slowly, arms set rigid and unnatural. He stalls four more times throughout the lesson and grinds the gearbox whenever he attempts a gear change. At the end of the lesson, he refuses to book another, thinking to himself I knew I would be a terrible driver, I can't do this.

Can you see how Ashley's negative thoughts created negative feelings, which in turn impacted his driving ability and reinforced the idea that he can't drive? Ashley is no different from anyone else. Perhaps you didn't struggle with driving, but I'm sure you've felt this way about something before. This negative cycle is a form of self-sabotage; when we think like this we take ourselves out of the game before it's even started – in other words, you have already decided that you've failed your goal before trying to achieve it. In which case, what was the point in setting a goal to begin with? We all have feelings of 'I can't' at some point in our lives but you can't let them rule you. Break the cycle!

Unbeknown to Ashley, everyone stalls on their first lesson and usually many more times after that. But in his head he's the world's worst driver, so how does he overcome this? How can he kick self-sabotage to the kerb? When you're stuck in that vicious cycle like Ashley with his driving or me during my postnatal depression, you need to separate your thoughts, feelings and behaviours and treat them all as individuals. It all starts with the thoughts, here are the three steps of the CBT cycle:

1. Thoughts turn into feelings
2. Feelings turn into behaviours
3. Behaviours reinforce thoughts

Twenty years later and Ashley is hobbling up the high street, heavy carrier bags in each hand, weighing him down from both sides. The rain comes pouring down and he is soaked through. Twice a week he struggles back from the shop, loaded up with groceries like a donkey, he has to go twice because he can't carry everything in one trip. He can't drive and his husband works late, so unless he wants to wait around for him, he has to walk. He absolutely hates food shopping, it's become the bane of his life. He knows life would be so much easier if he could drive.

On this fateful day, as Ashley battles the weather and makes this hellish trip for the umpteenth time, he decides enough is enough! He can no longer do this for the rest of his life, he needs to learn to drive. His husband had been telling him this for a long time, but all that ever did was annoy him. It's been affecting their relationship for years. Ashley is reliant on his husband to get around and has never been independent.

As I said earlier on, timing is everything, no one can tell you when it's time to change. The decision is yours, but be aware, your reluctance to change can negatively affect the people surrounding you. It's always easier to change when you feel on top of things than when everything is slipping away from you.

Ashley is still nervous about driving but this time he understands CBT and is using the methods to manage his thoughts, feelings and behaviours. Instead of thinking I can't drive, he says to himself I can't drive but I can learn how to. When thinking what if I crash? he starts thinking what if the lesson goes really well? What if I actually enjoy it? And then he rationalises his thoughts, he questions them: why would I crash? I've never crashed before, in fact, I don't know anyone who has crashed in their first lesson because the instructor has partial control of the car. This time when Ashley sits in the driving seat, he goes through these steps. He knows it's natural to be nervous and that actually everyone stalls when they learn to drive, it doesn't mean he is a bad driver, just that he's learning.

Don't let negative thoughts and feelings hold you back from getting what YOU want. It all comes back to the brain, the fight, flight or freeze. That inbuilt fear of rejection and failure that we all have, don't let it rule your life. Self-sabotage is the easy way out, it's the reason you set wishy-washy goals such as happiness and freedom because if you don't really know what it means then you can't fail. But let me tell you something else, it also means you can never really have it. Everyone has feelings of self-doubt at some point in their lives, getting caught up in the 'what if' game. What if this happens, what if that happens, what if it all goes wrong. So what? I can tell you that for most of us, the worst things that will ever come from going for what YOU want and grabbing life with both hands are cheeks reddened with embarrassment and a slight dent in your pride. Both a small risk to take in considering the other end of the scale, you could smash your goal and get everything you have ever wanted.

Mirror, Mirror!

Before I move on to the 'WE thing', I want to recap on what you have learned about yourself so far. Everything I have discussed with you up until this point has had one key purpose: to help you understand yourself and your goals. It's all been to help you grow a greater sense of self-awareness, to gain a stronger understanding of who you are, and what it all means. When you know who you are, it becomes a lot easier to know what YOU want and therefore actually get it! It makes sense, right?

We have covered a lot, let's take a minute to reflect and acknowledge how far you have already come since you picked up this book from the shelves, or clicked the 'buy it now' button.

I want you to conduct your own self-analysis. Imagine yourself as a superhero, what are your superpowers and vulnerabilities? Your superpowers can be anything from the ability to remember the lyrics to every song from The 1975, or the fact that you work well in a team. It doesn't matter how big or small it is, everyone is good at something. Use the left-hand side of the table below to write down everything you are good at, all your skills, talents, party tricks and strengths.

On the right side of the table, list your vulnerabilities. Nobody is good at everything, even Superman is weak when it comes to kryptonite. Think of things you would like to improve on. Remember your goals, what skills and abilities might you need to make them happen that you don't have? What behavioural traits do you have that could hold you back from getting what YOU want?

Remember the purpose of this activity is to reflect on everything you've learned so far. Think about what you know about your behaviour, mindset and WHY you want what you want. There are no wrong or right answers here, so list as much as you can, use an extra sheet of paper if you need to.

This should take you 5-10 minutes to complete

Superpowers	**Vulnerabilities**

The more self-aware you are, the easier it will become to get what you want. Knowing and acknowledging your vulnerabilities makes it harder for them to hold you back like they have done so many times before. Embrace what you have, use your superpowers and knowledge of your vulnerabilities to put preventative measures in place, don't let those same hurdles trip you up like they have in the past.

Mirror, mirror on the wall. Go and look at yourself in the mirror. Physically stand there and look at the person staring back at you.

What do you see? Who do you see?

Do you see all the superpowers that you just wrote down? Or do you see all the vulnerabilities that you wish you could change?

When you look at your reflection do you see yourself in the same way others see you? The answer is probably not. When you look in the mirror you see yourself from your own perspective; a lot of the time the way you see yourself will alter depending on your mindset and mood. One day you can look in the mirror and absolutely love what you see, yet the next day you may find it impossible to see past your flaws. I am sure you have experienced this, I know I certainly have.

Sometimes the way you view yourself can be the thing that holds you back from achieving your goals, stopping you from getting what you really want. I want to introduce you to something called Impostor syndrome. This is a term used when individuals have an inability to internalise their accomplishments and suffer from a persistent fear of being exposed as a 'fraud' or a 'fake'. Even when evidence proves their achievements, they find it difficult to take the credit and often dismiss their success as luck, timing or a result of making others think they are more intelligent and competent than they believe themselves to actually be.

Let me elaborate by sharing my own personal experience with Impostor syndrome. When I first started my business as a sales trainer, I had never actually been one before. I had mentored other salespeople and I had worked in corporate sales for years and I was good at it, you only had to look at my track record to see that. I knew I was good, and I wanted to share my knowledge and experience to help small businesses that didn't get access to the level of training I had received working for a multimillion pound company.

Thousands upon thousands of people start businesses doing things they love every day and I was no different. I love running my own business, but I had no experience, I didn't have a business degree. When I was with my clients, they saw me as the expert sales trainer, the specialist in my field. But what I saw when I looked in the mirror was something completely different. I wasn't a businesswoman or a sales trainer, so what was I? A fake, a phoney, someone just pretending. I was always waiting for someone to turn around and catch me out and see me for what I really was – an impostor who could talk a good game.

Whenever I think back to this time, there is one particular networking meeting that always springs to mind. During the early days of my business, my children were still fairly young, the only group I could make was an evening session when Neil was home from work to look after the kids.

Networking is a great way to meet new people, especially if you're a new business. I would go along with my two friends, Elaine and Emma, both of whom helped to organise the event. The group would gather regularly and because it was an evening meeting, it meant there was always wine. If you have never attended a networking group, they tend to follow a general format. Everyone gets 30 seconds or a minute to introduce themselves to the room, then perhaps there is a small presentation from a member. Finally, there is time for free networking, where you can go around and have a chat, the purpose of which is to obviously talk business, I mean that is why everyone is there isn't it?

Well almost everyone. I'll be honest with you. I wasn't there so much for the business as I was for the glass of wine, to have a natter to my friends and to get out of the house. I was a regular at the meeting, and when I first started going I went because I thought that's what business people did, and I was one of those now! Or was I? I mean I was just pretending, everyone else had real businesses.

One night Elaine and Emma said to me, "Alison, you should go talk to that guy, he said he wants some sales training." Were they joking!? I couldn't actually help him, I had no idea what I was doing, I was just pretending, remember? I said to them, "Oh no, he doesn't want me, he wants a 'real' sales trainer." To which they both looked at me and laughed. They had no clue what I was on about, in their eyes I was the real deal. Nevertheless, they thrust me in his direction.

I approached the man and had a chat. I was so nervous that I spent more time babbling about how I wasn't really a sales trainer than anything else. You can imagine his confusion. Goodness knows how but I did eventually end up working with him. Now, imagine how stunned I was to have actually bagged a client – me, someone who was just pretending. Many years later and we still laugh about that first meeting when I was a fumbling mess. Remember, what you see when you look in the mirror isn't always the same as what others see when they look at you. Don't be the one to hold YOU back.

My Impostor syndrome was really preventing me from making the most of those meetings. I probably passed up multiple opportunities to work with potential customers because I was always too scared that they would realise I wasn't like them and that actually I was just pretending.

I would compare myself to other people in my field, always thinking that they were better than me. I would feel bad for charging my clients money for my service, they shouldn't be paying me, I wasn't any more qualified than the next Tom, Dick or Harry. I would turn down clients because I had convinced myself that I wasn't good enough and they needed a 'real' sales trainer. My husband told me I was "playing at it". You might think this sounds a bit harsh but to be honest, he was right, I had let feelings of self-doubt hold me back from giving my business a real chance.

Running my own business had become my main ambition, at this point I wanted nothing more, how was I going to make it a success if I felt guilty every time I sent an invoice or delivered training? Now, years later, not only have I got an award-winning company, but I also received an MBE from the Queen for my services to Entrepreneurship and Small Business.

The only person undervaluing me was myself. This was a real turning point for me and when I discovered the ethos 'I think I am, therefore I am', which basically means if I believe in myself then I can do anything. When I believe it so do those around me. It's a little bit like a self-fulfilling prophecy. I don't necessarily mean fake it until you make it, I mean learn to have trust in yourself, believe in yourself, you are both your superpowers, vulnerabilities and so much more. Stop looking at your reflection and start seeing the whole picture.

Have you ever felt like this? Like you're not good enough and that someone would do a much better job than you? I'm sure you have. We all feel like this at some point. But what can you do to overcome these feelings?

1. **Mind Matters**

   The one thing that will always help is working on your mindset. Feelings of self-doubt and anxiety stem from fear, and as I have already said, the fixed mindset loves to use your fear against you. Managing your mindset is always going to be one of the most powerful things you can do to overcome low self-confidence. Revisit the SMASH IT! model and practise the process for overcoming internal objections.

2. **Every Superhero Has Their Kryptonite**

This is why we are working on building a strong sense of self-awareness. You know that you have both superpowers and vulnerabilities, everyone has downfalls, you are not the only one. At times when you can't see past the flaws remind yourself of your superpowers! They are always there, you just need to remind yourself sometimes.

3. **Think Positive**

This is easier said than done. Did you know that your brain pays more attention to the negative things in your life than the positive? It's called negative bias (Tierney, 2020). That's why we can always recall the insults rather than the compliments, and the reason you can have a really great day at work yet the only thing you will remember when you get home is the one bad thing that happened. What you can do is look for all the positives in your day. You could even ask a friend what they see when they look at you. This may seem scary, but you'll probably be knocked sideways when they respond, those around us usually see our superpowers a lot easier than we see ourselves. I know I have spoken a lot about self-esteem when discussing Maslow's and the difference between high and low. Although we all ultimately strive to achieve high esteem, receiving positive affirmations from others isn't necessarily a negative thing if it helps us get there.

4. **Flip It**

   When you do have a negative experience, it can be hard to see the silver lining. Referring back to the comment my husband Neil made, for many this would send them on the fast track to divorce. However, it was the kick in the backside I needed to realise that if I really wanted to make things work, I was going to have to change something. Nobody else could fix my problem, only me. It really does come back to having a growth mindset, a negative doesn't have to be negative, you can always flip it and learn from it.

5. **Stop Looking at Them**

   I have said it before and I will say it again, stop comparing yourself to others! You will never be them and they will never be you, that is what makes us all unique. The chances are, every time you try to be like someone else, there is another person trying to be just like you. Comparison is a vicious circle in which you can never win. Stop trying to be someone else because you think they are better, prettier, stronger or smarter. The world doesn't need another one of them, it just needs you to be YOU.

This is the part where a lot of personal development books stop, because they only look at YOU. They don't focus on the other external forces or people that affect your goals. We're now going to move on to the 'WE thing'. It's the combination of these that make this book unique.

THE
'WE THING'

TEAMWORK MAKES THE DREAM WORK

Everything I have covered up until this point has focused purely on you and what you can do to overcome the internal walls that stop you from getting what YOU want. But what do you do when you aren't the person that's stopping you from achieving your goals, what about when someone else is blocking you?

Should you just give up before you have even started? Maybe just change your goal to something easier? After all, there is no point worrying about something you have no control over, right? Wrong! You should never change your goals just because you think it's easier, all you will achieve by doing this are feelings of unfulfilment and dissatisfaction. As for not worrying about things you can't control, this is true, but when it comes to YOUR goals, YOU always have a say. Even when your goal is a 'WE thing', the outcome is still largely dependent on you and what you do. This is why it is important that you don't skip any steps; if you have categorised your goals into the 'WE thing' group, you still need to do everything I covered in the 'ME thing' section and then some.

When someone else is involved in your goals, you need to learn to work as a team. After all, teamwork does make the dream work. I have already shown you how to overcome internal objections and sell to yourself; in this section we are going to look at how you can use the same methods to communicate, cooperate and collaborate effectively with others in order to influence the situation and increase your chances of getting what YOU want.

This section will help you achieve goals that are based around relationships, careers and finance, including:

- Getting a job
- Buying and selling goods and services
- Getting married
- Receiving a promotion
- Asking for discounts
- Filing for divorce
- Starting a family

And everything in between. Any goal you have set that involves another person, whether it be selling your car, buying from a shop, or jumping into the dating pool, is a 'WE thing'. This section contains everything you need to know to ensure that no one gets in your way, giving you the tools to allow you to SMASH IT!

What is Adaptation?

According to Charles Darwin, adaption is the key to survival. We adapt our behaviour every day, most of the time without even realising. I like to think of us like chameleons, we change our behaviour to fit different environments. Again, this can be linked back to caveman times, when only the fittest would survive; by adapting your behaviour your brain is trying to protect you from any harm or embarrassment and increase your chances of survival. I have spoken a lot about finding your natural dominant behaviour and what this means for you in terms of goal achievement. Now I would like to explain further what I mean when I refer to the adapted behaviour.

This, however, is a natural response to your environment. But what if I told you that you can make an active choice to adapt your behaviour to build strong relationships with people who are not like you? Sometimes we see other people who are not the same as us as a barrier which prevents us from getting what we want. In this section, I'm going to give you the tools to get them on side to make the magic happen and get what YOU want! This may sound quite manipulative, but when it's done correctly it's a natural transition and it's a win-win for everybody.

If adapting your behaviour is something you do naturally, then why do you need to learn how to do it? As I said, adapting is a form of self-defence, it's a survival aid that our brains have perfected over many, many years. For most of us, we don't think about taking our hand off a hot plate, we just do it, that's very much the same with our behaviour. If you were going to eat dinner with the Queen, you don't really have to think about whether or not you're going to pick your food up with your hands and start scoffing your face like you do when you are sat at home eating dinner in front of the television, tuning into the latest episode of your favourite show. You know it's not appropriate and you reach for the cutlery without giving it a second thought, your brain has assessed the environment and made the decision for you, usually before you even know it. The reason it does all of this is to protect you.

But when you're trying to work with someone else, it's no longer all about you, it's about them too. Learning to adapt with purpose brings adaptation into the conscious and enables you to maximise the natural skills you have always had but don't always use. We are all brought up to treat others how WE would like to be treated; I challenge this statement and say treat others how THEY would like to be treated. It sounds odd but adapting to someone else actually makes it easier to get what YOU want.

I want to make it clear that there is a difference between adapting and acting. Adapting is utilising the skills you have to ensure you achieve the desired outcome from a particular situation. Think of it like playing golf. When you play golf you carry around a bag full of different clubs, ranging from drivers to a putter. Each club has a particular purpose; before taking a swing you will assess the distance to the hole, the conditions and any potential hazards that might get in your way. Based on these factors you will choose the appropriate club.

However, over time you start to develop favourites, in my case, I much prefer the 5 wood over the 3 iron, there's something about the familiar way it feels in my hands and the tried and trusted results it has produced in the past, which makes it my go-to club. However, there are times where my 5 wood just doesn't seem to cut the mustard. It's at times like this when I have to take a look in my bag at all my clubs and use one I haven't played with for a while. It feels a little rusty at first but it soon starts to feel right. I take the shot and it does the job. Once I'm done, I pop it back in my bag and finish the game using my trusty favourite clubs.

This is the same when you adapt your behaviour. You are a mixture of Red, Yellow, Green and Blue. You may be a dominant Red, but you still have the ability to be Green when you need to. The skills have always been in your bag, it's just you don't use them that much because they are not your favourites, they don't come as naturally as others. When we adapt, we tone down our dominant colour and make use of the others in order to achieve the desired outcome from the situation. Once you've achieved what you set out to do, you slip back into your default behaviour.

You see, the difference between adapting and pretending to be something you're not is that when you adapt you don't hide your dominant colour, you're just exercising one of the other behaviour types that you've always had but don't always use. Whereas when you act and pretend to be someone you are not, you want other people to think you're something else. For example, you try to make those around you think you're a high Yellow when in reality you're a high Green.

Acting in this way never lasts because it is physically and emotionally exhausting. Great examples of this are the television shows *Big Brother* or *Love Island*. When the contestants first go into the house they all want to be liked by everyone. They do what they can to act and look like the person they think everyone wants to see, doing whatever they can to make themselves likeable. But nobody can keep up this charade forever, as I said it is exhausting. A week in the house and the acts start to slip, friendships are formed, enemies are made and the fancy-dancy clothes and makeup are forgotten about. Their true colours start to show, and we get to know them for who they really are, not for what they wanted us to believe at the beginning.

You should always embrace who you really are. Adapt your behaviour when it is necessary but don't try to be someone else. If you're a high Red then be a high Red, but don't be afraid to tap into your Green side if and when needed. Remember you are and always will be a combination of all four colours.

Can you remember Grace, the young journalist from the beginning of the book? Grace was trying to hide her working-class background from her new middle-class friends, she would alter tiny details of information such as pretending she lived in a nicer area than she did. This isn't adapting. This is pretending. I told you at the beginning you don't have to change who you are and I still stand by that. When you adapt, the information that comes out of your mouth doesn't change but the way in which you deliver it does.

Think about when you go on holiday or speak to someone whose first language isn't the same as yours. You know what you want to say but if you blurt it out like you normally would they probably won't understand. Instead, you adjust your accent, you pronounce words and you talk at a slower pace. You might even use simpler words that are more recognisable. When you do this, do you think you're pretending to be something you are not? No, of course you don't.

That's the exact same when you adapt your behaviour, the purpose is to communicate effectively in a way that the other person can understand. You don't want them to misinterpret what you're saying like you don't want the man on the market stall on holiday to misinterpret you, therefore you adjust your speech and body language in a way that ensures the other person can better understand.

There is a thin line between adapting and acting, most people don't know where that line is and often overstep the mark. As we continue, I will teach you how to adapt with purpose, helping you to embrace your true colours and consciously alter your behaviour when you need to. Over-adapting or trying to be someone you're not takes a lot of energy; you'll probably find that if you do this a lot you will need to take a minute or two to recharge your batteries.

When you learn to adapt, it may seem a bit silly at first. It doesn't come naturally straight away, and your brain tells you that you look stupid or are making an embarrassment of yourself; it wants to protect you, so it tries to force you back into your natural behaviour where you feel comfortable. I'm telling you this because I want you to know that it's not easy and it does take a lot of time and practice to get to a place where you feel comfortable doing this. The more you do it, the easier it will become. This is why having a growth mindset is important, you need to be OK with messing up and learning from your mistakes until you get it right and be able to avoid the temptation to take the easy route because ultimately this will get you nowhere.

Knowing me, Knowing you

Before you can adapt your behaviour to other people to get what YOU want when your goal is a 'WE thing', you have to identify the other person's behaviours. If you can identify, you can influence. Maybe you want a holiday, and you are trying to convince a friend to go with you; maybe you are going for a promotion at work and need to show your boss you're the best for the job; or maybe you simply want your child to contribute more to the household chores. Whoever it is – it might be more than one person – you need to know exactly who they are.

You already have a good idea of what your behaviour style is, but what about that of the person you are trying to influence? Not everyone thinks the same way you do; you need to have an open mind and understand that the person you are talking to might not see things in the same way as you. I am going to show you how you can use your knowledge of the behaviours to increase effective communication, build stronger relationships, and ultimately get what YOU want! Understanding your own behaviour is one thing but understanding someone else's and knowing how to use this knowledge is another.

How do you know if someone is Red, Yellow, Green or Blue? In the previous section we spoke a lot about the traits and characteristics that you may exhibit. Here I am going to explain some more physical, observable traits which will help you tell the colours apart. This will make it easier for you to work out someone's dominant behaviour, providing you with deeper insights.

Again, at this point I will reiterate, do not label people one colour as we are a mix of all. This will help you to identify the colours in their purest forms. The purpose of this is to give you typical traits to look out for rather than providing an exact science. This system works particularly well when used correctly but can backfire if not.

An area that I specialise in is identifying colours on LinkedIn, the business networking tool. From this we can identify the behaviours based on somebody's photo and profile, as covered in my previous book. Social media allows us to be whoever and whatever we want. Introverts can come across as the most extroverted people online, it gives them a face and a voice that they wouldn't necessarily use in the real world. On Twitter, they're keyboard warriors but in real life they wouldn't say boo to a goose. On Instagram, they are living their best #girlboss life whilst in real life they would struggle to start a conversation. For that reason, it becomes almost impossible to identify the behaviours via social media, so I won't be covering it. If you want to know how to identify on LinkedIn, take a look at my first book for all of the answers.

I'll be teaching you how you can identify somebody in the following situations:

- Face to face looking at their communication both verbally and through their body language
- Virtual: due to the COVID-19 pandemic we have transitioned a lot of our communication to the virtual world. My prediction for the future is that we will continue with some of the virtual working practices, meaning it's a good idea to understand how to identify the behaviour types via

Zoom, Teams, Skype or any other virtual communication tool

- Written communication: how do they text or DM? How do they email?

How do you identify someone's RED behaviours?

Face to Face

- Straight posture to make them look taller and bigger
- Firm handshake (COVID-19 dependent!) and/or a strong introduction
- Strong eye contact
- Leans forward when interested
- Looking around to see who is looking at them
- Checks watch or clock for time
- Will start checking phone and doing other things they deem to be more important when disengaged
- Interrupts conversation to share their opinion, especially when interested
- Likely to be wearing something classic and potentially pared-back designer

Virtual

- Preference for camera on
- Will be on time and expect meeting to finish promptly (applies to face to face too)
- Will take control of the meeting agenda (applies to face to face too)

- Will either have a professional background or awards
- Show frustration when somebody doesn't know how to work the tech

Written and Messaging

- Bullet point communication
- Abbreviations like FYI (for your information) and TL, DR (too long, didn't read)
- No pleasantries, they won't ask how your weekend was
- One-word answers
- Short, concise, to the point

Some people would perceive Red behaviour as being rude, especially if you're Green. This is because they're focused on getting the task completed. They will make it clear when they are not interested or have better things to do; they don't necessarily mean for this to be rude, it's just that they are task-focused, so they see their time as precious.

How do you identify someone's YELLOW behaviours?

Face to Face

- Big, expressive hand gestures
- Smiley face and very expressive
- Touchy feely, lots of hugs and cheek kisses on arrival
- Looking around the room to see who else is there
- Easily distracted by phone notifications
- Talks fast and loudly

- Likely to be wearing something loud with big designer labels

Virtual

- Preference for camera on
- Likely to be late and will burst in loud
- Will distract from the agenda, wanting to talk about themselves
- Either a virtual background of a holiday they've been on or showing off their house
- May be faffing around with the tech
- Obviously distracted, often on their phone texting or flicking through other browser tabs/emails
- Taking a photo of the meeting to post on their Instagram story

Written and Messaging

- Use a lot of emojis, GIFS and kisses
- Words like hun, babe or mate
- Use I a lot, telling stories about themselves
- Forget they've already messaged you about the same thing
- Machine-gun messages, rather than sending one paragraph they will send multiple messages

I always think of the Yellows as having jazz hands. They wave their hands around a lot when they are trying to get their point across. They aim to influence; when the Yellows look around the room, they are looking to see who else they know and can strike up a conversation with, not because they aren't interested in what you have to say but because they want to be the most popular person in the room. Yellows are also relationship-focused so are interested in other people, just not as much as themselves! They are intuitive, which comes across in their very expressive movements and facial gestures as well as their tactile nature.

How do you identify someone's GREEN behaviours?

Face to Face

- Position in the room will be somewhere quiet or unnoticeable
- Arms crossed to act as a barrier
- Avoids direct eye contact when nervous
- Welcoming and warm smile
- Nod head to show they are listening and engaged
- Softer tone of voice
- Slower and more thoughtful with their words
- Fiddles with things when nervous
- Touchy feely, shoulder patting and hugging
- Wear muted colours because they don't want to stand out

Virtual

- Preference for camera off
- May be late due to 'personal circumstances' because they have been helping someone else
- Lead with an apology, even if there's nothing to apologise for (both face to face and virtual)
- Will avoid talking and spend more time listening

- If they have to have their camera on, they will have pictures of their family or children's drawings in the background; may opt for a plain virtual background
- Potentially nervous of the tech and apologising in advance for any lack of knowledge
- Show that they're listening by nodding, may raise their hand before they speak

Written and Messaging

- Always open with pleasantries: 'I hope you're well!', 'How was your weekend?', 'How are the family?'
- Always sign off with a meaningful goodbye, 'Warm regards', 'Have a great day!'
- Over-apologetic, 'I'm sure you're busy', 'Sorry for bothering you'
- Will remember key meaningful details that you may have mentioned before
- May use subtle emojis or a kiss

As introverts, someone who is a high Green will shy away from the spotlight; in a crowded room they will position themselves on the edge, often looking a little lost. When nervous and meeting someone for the first time, a Green will fumble and stumble over their words and can sometimes appear as though they are shrinking into themselves. However, once comfortable you'll soon see their relationship-focused side, they will become more tactile and will begin making more eye contact. Their voices usually remain soft and delicate, but they will carry their words with more confidence. They feel comfortable when they are surrounded by small groups, allowing them to feel secure.

How do you identify someone's BLUE behaviours?

Face to Face

- Avoids eye contact
- Struggle to start a conversation, but when you get them talking, they want to tell you all of the details about a specific subject
- Not expressive, their faces are very hard to read
- Eloquent and succinct speech
- Tactile averse
- Formally dressed perhaps with a suit and tie or, when dressed down, no designer clothes because they like value for money!

Virtual

- Preference for camera off
- Will be on time (applicable to face to face)
- Will prepare a strict agenda and will not be afraid to pull you up if you deviate away from the conversation (applicable to face to face)
- Will give you all of the details at the appropriate time
- If they have to have their camera on, their background will be based around their company's standard operating procedure
- Know the tech like the back of their hand, internally will be infuriated at anybody who isn't as thorough as them

Written and Messaging

- Much more formal even when communication via DM, won't necessarily lead with pleasantries: 'Further to our last conversation I'd like to confirm…'

- All communication task-led
- Long emails or messages with a lot of minute details and attachments
- NO emojis or kisses!

The Blues don't give a lot away with their body language, which I actually think is what makes them easy to recognise. They are introverts; unlike the extroverted Reds and Yellows, their actions and expressions are very minimal. If you are ever speaking to someone and you find they are completely hard to read, then it's most likely you are talking to a Blue. I always think of the Blues having the ultimate poker face. As task-focused introverts, they may come across as very formal and intolerant of extroverted people, but that's just because they don't know how to adapt.

If you pair together the information you learned about the behaviour in the previous section with your new knowledge of how to identify the colours, you should be able to make a fairly informed decision regarding someone's behaviour. It will be easier to interpret some individuals' behaviour than others, but you will get better with practice. I will remind you that analysing someone's behaviour is not 100% accurate and the only way to truly know is through official testing. One thing is for sure, if other people are involved, this knowledge is key for getting what YOU want.

CASE STUDY: MEET TESS AND JESSIE...

The Situation

Tess and Jessie are mother and daughter. Tess has a psychology degree and is a former social worker. Jessie is Tess's 16-year-old daughter, she has just finished school and is about to start her first year at college. Each person has their own goal. As a mother, Tess just wants the best for her child and to get through that stubborn teenage stage with as little stress as possible. Jessie on the other hand just wants to get through school life without sticking out too much.

The Problem

As someone with a background in psychology, Tess has a good understanding of the behaviours and how they work, yet she was still struggling to communicate with Jessie and find a middle ground. As a teenager in her final year of school, Jessie was under a lot of pressure. "School is different from when I was young, with social media and emails there is no escape, school literally invades your home," said Tess. Not only was it the constant emails from teachers outside of school hours that overwhelmed Jessie, but also the jibes and mean comments on social media from classmates made her feel not good enough.

As a parent, one of Tess's biggest concerns was how Jessie was coping at school, she had never been overly confident and sometimes struggled with the other pupils. Jessie couldn't understand why some people acted in the way they did and why this made her feel negative about herself.

Tess had tried to sit down with Jessie and use her knowledge of psychology to explain why people are the way they are, but as a stubborn 16-year-old, Jessie wasn't ready to listen and quite often their talks would end up in arguments with neither of them feeling like the other person listened or understood. Tess could see that the negativity from teachers and pupils at school was really beginning to impact Jessie's self-esteem and confidence. She had started to become very anxious to the point where she didn't want to get the bus or walk home from school, Tess would have to pick her up every day.

The Win-Win

Tess had come across Alison's book and despite not being in sales had heard that it had an interesting take on human psychology. She would listen to the e-book aloud on her Amazon Alexa, often while Jessie was around. When it got to the behaviours section of the book, Tess noticed that Jessie was actively listening and started to ask more questions about what the colours meant.

It was at this point that Tess decided to buy the paperback book for her daughter so she could read it for herself. "At first, she was apprehensive, I think having heard a little bit of the book already, she wanted to know more but was a little put off by the title. I said to not judge a book by its cover as I think there's lots in there that could be helpful."

"I knew she was reading the book because I saw the bookmark move, but she hadn't mentioned anything for a while. Then one day she came home and was telling me about a bad lesson with her maths teacher and explained to me how she knew her teacher was like this because she had Red behaviours."

Over the next four to five months is when Tess really saw the difference in Jessie. She said she noticed that she was referring more and more to the colours and even the communication between the two of them had improved. The newly found mutual interest and understanding that the pair had around human behaviour had strengthened their bond.

One year later and Jessie is like a different person. When it came to choosing further education, she chose to attend a college away from home as it could provide her with better schooling and stronger job prospects. Despite teachers telling her that she would be hard pushed to make it into a low-level course at that particular college, she didn't give up and managed to talk herself into earning a place on the higher-level course. Tess said, "I was relieved after Jessie read the book, it's like she had all of a sudden found herself and a new sense of confidence."

The Techniques

The main thing that Tess did was recognise that although she knew the psychology of the behaviours, she wasn't necessarily applying them to her home life. When she started adapting to Jessie and seeing things from her point of view it became easier to help her. In a way she used *Secrets of Successful Sales* almost as a parenting tool; before she would try and explain the information to Jessie but she wouldn't listen. Sometimes when the relationship is so close it can be tough to take advice; by giving her the book, Tess could give Jessie the advice without having to physically tell her.

It's advised that individuals under the age of 18 don't undertake a behaviour profiling test until they have finished growing and developing. However, for Jessie just understanding why people behave differently was already enough to make a massive difference in her life. When she was able to rationalise why her teachers and classmates said things and acted in the way they did, she realised that it actually wasn't about her. In fact, it said more about who they were than anything else. In turn this helped her to overcome negative comments in a more positive way.

The other thing that Jessie really took from the book were lessons of confidence and mindset. Despite being told she had slim chances of being accepted into college, she didn't let that dampen her dreams. In fact, she pushed even harder and became a fantastic example of 'I think I am, therefore I am'.

Adapting with Purpose

If you have identified one of your goals as being a 'WE thing', what I am about to share with you is the single most important thing that will help you influence the situation and achieve your desired outcome.

For me, this part of the book is one of the most fundamental things you can take away, and I want to do my best to convey my passion for its importance. I'm sure you might be thinking well why should I adapt? Other people should be more understanding of my feelings and they should be more like me! The key word here is **feelings**. It's the relationship-focused colours who wear their hearts on their sleeves. For the task-focused behaviours, it's not that they don't have feelings, it's that the task holds more precedence for them. They are naturally wired to push their emotions aside to get the task done.

The truth is, everybody needs to adapt, but until everybody has read my book and understands the behaviours, it's gotta be YOU! After all, this book is about getting what YOU want. You can set as many goals as you want; if it's a 'ME thing' they can be achievable without adaptation, but if any of your goals are 'WE things' adaptation is INTEGRAL! My secret is don't change who you are, change how you behave.

Sometimes, if you are not a Red you can see them as being mean. And, in all honesty, every behaviour type has the capacity to behave that way. One of the fundamental things is to remember that you can't control how somebody else behaves, the only thing you can control is how you react to it.

There is a lot of talk around kindness at the moment, especially across social media. I feel if everyone was kind, the world would be a much better place. But in all honesty, you can't control whether somebody else is kind or not. What you can control is how you react to it. You can control how resilient you are to people who are not kind because quite often people don't realise they're being rude or harsh because they aren't self-aware. This may seem annoying and unfair, and not how things should be, but unfortunately because you are the one who is self-aware, you have to adapt and accept.

Not everyone thinks in the same way as you do, the four behavioural styles are evidence of this. When working with someone else, whether it be in a personal or professional relationship, cooperation is key. To cooperate, you have to understand the other person's point of view. As the old adage goes, you have to put yourself in their shoes. I am going to show you how you can take your knowledge of the behaviours and use it to create effective communication and ultimately get what YOU want.

It's all about adapting and appealing to someone's better nature. Let me be clear, this is not a case of 'fake it until you make it' but adapt when apt. It's about assessing your environment, being perceptive and finding the best way to work with someone. It's about utilising all the clubs in your golf bag, not just your favourites.

There are lots of times in life when you won't need to adapt at all, this is because like finds like. By this I mean we are naturally drawn to people who are like us. When you are trying to work with someone who thinks the same way as you, it's always going to be easier than when someone is the polar opposite. I am going to show how to communicate with those who are not like you, how you can adapt your approach and convince them to help you get what YOU want!

How to get what YOU want with RED behaviour types

Adapt Your Pace

It may be true in the case of the Tortoise and the Hare, but for the Reds, slow and steady doesn't win the race. Instead, you need to be concise and to the point. Reds are task-focused and time conscious, they make decisions fast. If you're a high Green, you might find that you're naturally a slower talker. This doesn't mean you have to start speaking at 100 miles per hour, it just means you have to keep your words clear and succinct.

You may feel intimidated by the Reds and resort to apologising. My top tip is DO NOT DO THIS! As soon as you start wasting their time (in their eyes) by saying things like 'I'm sorry to bother you', you'll lose them. If you are a high Blue, this is something you might also struggle with, as your tendency to dive into detail might come across as time-wasting to a Red. The secret is to drop the waffle and cut to the chase. If you don't get there quickly, you will have lost the ability to work with the Red to get what YOU want.

Focus on the Tasks/Facts, not the Feelings

Adapting to Reds is difficult, especially when you're relationship-focused. Where you would naturally focus on your feelings, the Reds just want to know the facts and keep things focused on the task. When you're asking for something, they don't want to hear a story of all of your hardships, they just want you to get to the point. It's not because the Reds don't care about your feelings, it's just that they view their time as precious and are keen to get the conversation over and done with so they can return to the Basketball in hand.

Lead the Dance

Reds like to dominate the situations, that's their natural reaction, remember? When it comes to speaking to a Red, you have to be the one to take control, I call it leading the dance. It takes two to tango but only one can lead, and it's usually the Reds who want to do so. If you let them take control, they will get what they want, leaving you as the passenger and people pleaser. You will walk away scratching your head and wondering what just happened.

After you've told them what YOU want, you need to give them a clear plan of how you can work together to get there. This means you're not only offering what Reds would see as a problem, but you are also giving them the solution. By doing this, you're playing to their weaknesses. Reds hate an unfinished task! Being in control doesn't mean banging on your chest and proving you're the alpha male, all you have to do is have a clear plan and execute it properly. I'll give you some more tips on how you can do this in the next section.

CASE STUDY: MEET MARK...

The Situation

Mark is a 20-something IT technician. He loves what he does, computers have always been his thing, but he hates going to work. Mark wants the same as so many others, he wants to enjoy his job, or at least not dread it every morning.

The Problem

The main thing that stops Mark from enjoying work is his manager. He has to report to her on a regular basis and no matter what he does, she is always aggressive towards him. She is impatient, abrupt, and Mark just can't seem to do anything right. Sometimes he feels she is on the verge of bullying him. She is constantly nagging him about deadlines and despite his constant explaining, she doesn't seem to understand that certain jobs take time.

He is sick and tired of the overwhelming feeling of anxiety that he feels in the pit of his stomach on his commute to work. Every day when he wakes up, the thought of having to face his manager again fills him with dread and he just wants to roll over and bury his head beneath the covers. The moment he leaves the office, a wave of relief washes over him, knowing that he has made it through another day, but this doesn't last long before the sickening feeling comes back as he thinks about what the next day might bring.

He really likes being an IT technician and has created some strong relationships with the rest of the team, he would be sad to leave them. He knows that no job is perfect and worries that if he leaves he could be in the same situation again with someone else without the support of his colleagues. He feels like he is stuck between a rock and a hard place. He knows he really only has two choices: find a way to work with his manager or find another job.

The Win-Win

Mark knew that if he was going to get on with his manager, something had to change. With my help, he learned about the different behaviour types, instantly things started to make sense.

Mark knew he couldn't change his manager's behaviour, but he could do something about his own. The next time he met with his manager he tried to speak clearly and confidently about his role in the project. He kept it short and sharp, highlighting the key details he knew his manager wanted to know and emphasised the project deadline. For the first time, Mark noticed that his manager had very little to criticise.

Now when he communicates with her, he suppresses his natural urge to over-apologise and explain the technicalities behind his work, sticking to the key information he thinks she wants to hear. Mark realised that by doing this, his manager had less information to pick holes in. She also seemed to be more accepting of the deadlines than before. When they do have a disagreement, Mark tries not to take it too personally; recognising that his manager has Red behaviour, he now knows that her abrupt and aggressive manner isn't as a result of anything he has done, but because she is task-focused.

After trialling this new approach for several months, Mark decided not to look for another job. His anxiety had reduced and he didn't completely dread going to work anymore. He was actually starting to enjoy it again, he felt his manager understood him better and their working relationship had vastly improved, they even started going for walks during their lunch break. Mark's attitude towards work had greatly improved and his manager was happy with his performance, all she ever really wanted was to get the job done in an accurate and timely fashion and this was happening.

The Techniques

During my workshop, Mark identified himself with Blue/Green behaviours and his manager with Red/Yellow. These two combinations are complete opposites. Where she thought she was being efficient, Mark interpreted it as being officious. He learned that she wasn't really aggressive, in fact, she probably didn't realise she came across this way and he shouldn't take what she says personally. He learned that when dealing with a Red, sometimes you have to grow a thicker skin as they aren't always aware that what they are saying can be hurtful.

If I was training a team, I would say that everyone needs to make the effort to understand each other and adapt where necessary, but in everyday life this isn't possible. Not everyone will read this book, as much as I would love them to, which means whether you like it or not, you have to be the one to adapt. Mark adapted to meet his manager, he limited the technical detail knowing that this isn't of concern to someone who exhibits Red/Yellow behaviour, instead focusing on the key details his manager would want to know, such as deadlines. She is task-focused, therefore time will always be an important factor for her. He also worked on his delivery; it wasn't easy but he tried to match her body language, instead of shying away, he became confident and concise when communicating.

The key things Mark learned were if he was confident in himself, his manager would be confident in him, and a deeper understanding of behaviours which allowed him to treat other people the way THEY want to be treated and how it is useful to getting to what YOU want.

How to get what YOU want with YELLOW behaviour types

Get in Touch with Your Feelings

The Yellows are people people! As much as it might make you want to vomit in a bucket, you have to get in touch with your feelings and let them know how much their help in achieving your goal means to you. Because Yellows are well connected, they hold a lot of power in social situations as well as within the workplace. Remember, their focus is influence. They are a great catalyst to help get you what you want, especially if you have a good relationship with them.

Keep it Punchy, Expressive and SMILE!

The biggest challenge for anyone trying to bond with a Yellow is getting them to stand still and keep their mouths shut for long enough to actually listen to what you're saying! When adapting to Yellow, it's very much a case of keeping it simple. This is where you may struggle if you are a high Blue. If you start rambling on about the ins and outs, it's highly likely that the Yellow's eyes will glaze over, they will stop listening, and get distracted by their phone or something else in the room. Because a Blue is task-focused, they guard their emotions. The secret is to dig deep and be passionate about what you're saying, remember to smile, and keep them engaged. Share with them enough so that they can get on the same page but not so much that they feel overloaded and overwhelmed with information.

Allow Them to Feel in Control, but be in Control

Yellows like to be able to express themselves and share their thoughts and opinions. They also like to talk. A good way to keep them interested and engaged is by getting them involved straight away. Ask them what their thoughts are in regards to what you are saying, they will jump at the opportunity to give you their two pennies worth. Remember the Yellows aim to influence, letting them have their say gives them an opportunity to influence you, which they will thrive off. It allows them to feel as though they are driving the conversation, but remember they will dominate if you let them. You can steer things by asking closed questions, which will make them talk less, we'll come back to this later.

How to get what YOU want with GREEN behaviour types

Slow It Down

For the more fast-paced extroverts, sometimes communicating with a Green can be tough. Someone who is a high Green will naturally take more time to make decisions and will be hesitant about jumping in headfirst. However, given time, a Green can be confident and trust the decisions they make. This means when adapting to a Green, you need to slow down and practise the art of patience. Don't rush them into making a decision on the spot because they won't like that. Let them know that you understand they need to take their time and think things through.

As well as slowing down the conversation, you need to tone down your body language. This isn't such a problem for Blue behaviour types but can be challenging for a Red and Yellow. If you're a Red, your body language can often come across as intimidating to someone who is high Green. Try to relax your shoulders and soften your tone of voice, this will help make your words sound less abrupt. Yellows often speak so fast that they can send a Green into overwhelm, slow down your pace. Take a minute to pause and breathe between sentences, this will give a Green a chance to catch up with what you're saying before you move on to the next thing. Eye contact can be a tricky thing to get right when dealing with a Green; too much and they feel like you're trying to overpower them, too little and they think you're avoiding their gaze which will result in a lack of trust. My advice here is to let the Green lead and for you to reciprocate accordingly.

Be Genuine and Friendly

For the Greens, the most important thing for them is the details. Not facts and figures like the Blues, but the key details about them.

Things like their kids' names, their birthday, their anniversary with the company if they are your colleague. This is what I mean when I say be genuine, you need to understand the importance of these details to them. When you show a genuine interest, you are showing them that they matter, which means they are more likely to cooperate with you to get what YOU want!

How many times have you asked somebody how they are, and they've responded 'fine'? My top tip to work with the Greens is to use a scaling system, questions like, 'How do you feel on a scale of 1-5?' This is something I do with my team every day. This shows them that you care, and it allows them to open up too. Be careful though, once you open the can of worms, the Greens may spill all. This is a great way to build a relationship, showing genuine concern; however, naturally as a task-focused behaviour, you may feel the need to provide a solution to their issues, which can alienate the Greens as they don't see things the same way as you do. The key is to just be there to support, ask open questions like 'How can I help?'. I'll come back to questions later. To get what you want with a Green, you need to build a genuine relationship built on trust.

Give them Time

Finally, remember that Greens like to talk things out with a third party before making real decisions. This isn't because they want someone to make the decision for them, it's just they need an unbiased sounding board to help them organise their thoughts and feelings. I've already mentioned the importance of giving Greens time to process, another thing you can do to make it easier is to make whatever you're suggesting inclusive, if possible. Let them know that it's OK if they want to get someone else involved if it makes them feel more comfortable.

CASE STUDY: MEET JO...

The Situation

We met Jo earlier on in the book. Can you remember? Jo started her business so that she could have a career that worked around her children. She wanted what so many others do: a healthy work-life balance and financial freedom.

Previously I told you how Jo had built on her SMART goals by breaking them down into smaller actionable tasks that she could do every day. I will now continue with Jo's journey and highlight how she used my methods to progress further.

The Problem

One of the key issues Jo was struggling with was that some of her big goals were largely dependent on others. As a business owner, Jo had to work with different types of people all the time. Growing her business to achieve the financial freedom she had dreamed off meant having to work with more and more people. The thing that frustrated her most was that her team didn't seem to care about the end goal in the same way she did. They were holding her back; as the owner of the business, she needed them to hit their targets so that she could hit her own financial goals. The longer it took them, the longer it would take her, and this was something that was becoming increasingly irritating for Jo.

She knew it was her job to motivate and inspire them, but it seemed that no matter what she did, she couldn't get through to them. They just didn't care in the same way she did which made her question whether these were the right people to be working with.

The Win-Win

Jo had learned personality traits and different behaviours a million times before, but she had never really understood how to apply it until she worked with Alison. Jo exhibits strong Red behaviour but her team consisted of a lot of high Green behaviour. These two colours are the exact opposite. The problem Jo was having is that what she thought was inspiring and motivating was interpreted by a lot of her team as forceful and pushy. There is a thin line between assertive and aggressive, with such a wide range of people this line was difficult to find.

As a Red, Jo moves at a fast pace. She thought that bringing high energy to group meetings would energise the team and give them the va-va-voom needed to hit the ground running. But in reality, her team of high Greens felt overwhelmed and pressurised by this. Therefore, it was having the reverse effect that Jo intended.

To overcome this, Jo learned about how she can adapt her own behaviour in a way that meets both her needs and her team's. She changed the way she communicated with them. One of the ways she did this was by introducing more one-to-one conversations about individual performance rather than group meetings and discussions. As relationship-focused introverts, people who are high Green will respond better to a personal meeting over a blanket group one. Doing this also made it easier for Jo to adapt accordingly, as it meant she could work with each individual person's behaviour instead of feeling overwhelmed and trying to find a way that worked for everyone. She slowed down the pace for her team, realising that just because she likes things fast and loud, not everyone is motivated in the same way.

"I learned that one size doesn't fit all and to empower my team I needed to manage them how they wanted to be managed, not how I wanted to manage them. I can't be a Red with everyone because it doesn't work."

As a result of the changes Jo made, she saw an increase in the team's performance, focus, but most importantly their morale. For Jo, this had been a successful outcome, she felt like her team were now working as one to move closer towards their common goals and the team felt empowered and happier in their roles.

The Techniques

Jo embraced the behaviours unlike anyone I have ever seen. One of the biggest challenges when learning about colours and adaption is accepting that your way is not necessarily the right way. Jo took this in her stride and was quick to identify where her own behaviour might be clashing with that of those on her team. Developing the one-to-one relationships with her team members was a real turning point, as this benefited her two-fold. Firstly, it meant she could treat each individual how they want to be treated which made them feel understood and heard. Secondly, it actually made it easier for her to adapt. Adapting is tough at the best of times but trying to do it to multiple people is really difficult; focusing on the individuals made it easier for her to convert to this way of thinking.

Learning about the behaviours was a real game changer for Jo because it showed her that not only were the people in her team the right people to work with but also she could work with anyone once she knew how.

How to get what YOU want with BLUE behaviour types

Be Prepared, Do Your Research, and Listen Up!

My biggest piece of advice when dealing with anyone who is a high Blue is to make sure you are prepared. With the Blues, it is very much a case of 'fail to plan and you plan to fail'. For those that are high Yellow, this will be difficult for you, in depth planning just isn't in your nature. But when it comes to working the Blues, it's an absolute must. If you want to win them over, you'll need to tell them exactly what they are getting themselves into from the very beginning. And make sure you have done your research, because they will most definitely come back at you with a list of questions as long as your arm. If you can listen to what they're saying, hold your own, and answer all of their questions, they will take your proposal seriously. There's no 'winging it' when it comes to the Blues, they will find this offensive and rip you apart!

Have Proof, and Know the Details

Blues like to see proof, so if you can, always have something on hand to back up what you're saying. Even if you're trying to convince a high Blue to go on holiday with you, have the hotel resort guide ready, and print out the flight deals. Wherever possible, always provide them with physical proof that you have done your research. Blues would like to take physical proof away with them and read it at their own leisure. They will use it as a starting point to conduct their own research into the topic and see if they can uncover anything that you have missed. Even when you win them over, they will still conduct thorough research to ensure they are the most informed on the subject matter.

Respect Their Space and Tone It Down!

Someone who is a dominant Blue is very reserved with their emotions, hence why they are so hard to read. This is something that relationship-focused colours such as Yellow or Green might struggle with. Blues do not want to be faffed over, they don't want to be hugged or patted, they value their personal space. Try to respect their boundaries and keep any unnecessary physical contact to a minimum. Yellows, this might mean sitting on your hands rather than your usual jazz hands! Yellows will think that they can keep talking and use their influence to convince as they do with other behaviour types, but the Blues are much more likely to respect you and give you the time of day if you tone it down and respect them.

Treat Others How THEY Want to Be Treated

If you follow the tips and advice I have given you here, you will see that by making some adjustments to your behaviour, communication becomes more effective and relationships become stronger. Both of these will go a long way in helping you achieve your goals, especially when your goals include the participation of another person.

Before I move on, I want to reiterate again the importance of understanding the difference between adapting and acting. Usually before I share this knowledge with others, they think that by adapting they are being fake and phoney, but that's not the case. You should never feel like you're pretending to be someone else. What it actually means is that you have an open mind, therefore respect and understand that not everyone sees the world in the same way as you.

Every day of our lives, we automatically adapt to our surroundings, it's subconscious, but when you have little control over your behaviour you don't always achieve the desired outcome. Start consciously thinking about your behaviour and the impact it has on the people in your environment, make use of all elements of your behaviour, not just the parts you favour. Remember, **treat others how THEY want to be treated, not how YOU want to be treated**. We are not all the same, respect our individuality. This will enable you to get what YOU want!

SMASH IT! - THE 'WE THING'

Remember Matt from the SMASH IT! model in the 'Me thing'? He had to converse with himself to get what he wanted. You've now learned how to adapt your behaviour to build stronger relationships. This section will show you how you can utilise that adaptation combined with some ways to structure conversations to get what YOU want. You may recognise the method because actually the process of convincing yourself and somebody else is exactly the same. I'm going to walk you through step by step, teaching you how to get what YOU want when your goals involve other people.

Throughout this section, I will ask you to complete the tasks to help you practise each step of the process. However, this doesn't mean you can use your task answers as a script as this won't work in real life. When you are going through the process in a real-life situation, you will transition through each step naturally as the conversation and relationship progress. If you try to use a script, it will come off as disingenuous, a bit like when you get a cold caller and you can tell that they are more focused on trying to get through their predetermined script than actually listening to what you as the supposed 'customer' wants.

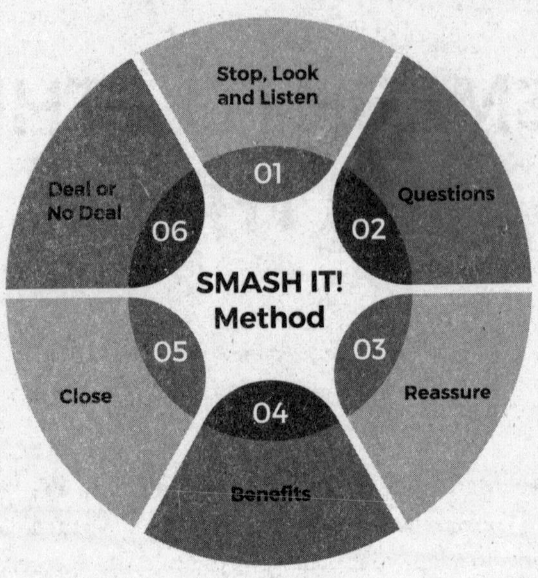

I have used a lot of examples throughout this book to help illustrate my theory, from weight loss to finding a job, to going on holiday. Another example that I haven't really touched on is around romantic relationships, which is a huge point of contention for a lot of people and may be something that you set as a goal at the start of the book. As I mentioned earlier, according to the Office of National Statistics, 38% of marriages in the year that I got married, 1997, have now ended in divorce. That's why, throughout this section, I want to use the example of Helen and Nigel to demonstrate that my method really can help you get what YOU want.

If you are, however, one of the lucky ones who are in a healthy relationship, you may think that this section is not relevant to you. But this process can be used in all situations when working with somebody to get what YOU want, this is just my way of contextualising. I am not a relationship counsellor, if you feel you need specialist help in this area there are organisations like RELATE who you can contact. The purpose of this example is to show you how my method works for all types of goals. So, without any further ado, let me introduce you to Helen and Nigel.

Helen is a 37-year-old mum of two to 10-year-old Zoe and eight-year-old Tom. She met her first husband, Gary, at university when she was 19; two kids and a 16-year marriage later and her life wasn't quite where she thought it would be. While she had thrown herself into parenthood, Gary had always struggled. When they first met, Helen loved that Gary was full of life, she enjoyed spending evenings at the pub with him and all their other mates, drinking pints until early hours in the morning and waking up at midday with no worries in the world. But they were teenagers then. As parents they have responsibilities and two amazing children that they absolutely adore.

For Helen stepping into the role of mum had been easy, her babies had brought a new meaning into her life. Although Gary loved the kids, he still wanted to watch the footie in the pub with the lads and spend all Sunday in bed recovering. Helen thought that Gary would grow out of this, after all, this was the life they had chosen together. Eventually, Helen got fed up with her and the kids playing second fiddle to *Match of the Day* and made the decision to walk away from the relationship.

The transition to being a single mum wasn't easy, but two years later and Helen and the kids are doing great! They have settled into a steady routine and everything with Gary has been rather amicable; together they were able to come up with an agreement that ensures they both get to spend equal time with Zoe and Tom.

As much as Helen loves her children, she has missed the company of an adult. She yearns for an intimate and mature romantic relationship, something that she feels has been missing from her life for many years even throughout her marriage to Gary. Helen has set a goal to try and find a new partner to share her life with before she turns 40, she wants someone who shares the same values as her and can fulfil her need for love and belonging. Putting herself back out in the dating world was a scary prospect and after a few dodgy dates she was starting to give up hope, that was until she met Nigel.

Nigel is a 42-year-old single parent to 11-year-old Harry after his wife left him for one of her colleagues from work. The past year since the divorce has been tough on Nigel, his relationship with his ex-wife is very volatile and has left him scarred. He wasn't even sure he was ready for another relationship when his friends encouraged him to sign up to one of those dating apps. He was reluctantly swiping through potentials when he matched with Helen. He wasn't even sure he was going to go on the date at first but figured he didn't have much to lose.

After their first date, Helen and Nigel really hit it off. They have now been together for six months. Nigel is steady, dependable and thoughtful, everything Helen was looking for in a relationship. Not only that but their kids get on great, which was one of Helen's biggest worries in the early stages.

Since her divorce, Helen has been renting a house but her lease is coming to an end. She could just renew her lease but that's not what she wants. She wants to move in with Nigel. To her it makes sense, they are always packing bags and moving from one house to the other, it would be easier if they moved in together. Not only that, but they could spend more time together and make the most of alone time when Zoe and Tom are with Gary and Harry is with his mother. However, Nigel seems reluctant. Helen can understand this considering his previous relationship, but she needs to make a decision about where she and the kids are going to live, she will not let them play second fiddle again.

Using the process, I am going to show you how achieving a win-win situation helps you get what you want.

Stop, Look and Listen

Remember Matt who worked in the electrical goods retailer from the 'ME thing' section? Can you remember when he was trying to convince himself to take growth actions? The first thing he needed to do was listen to the voice in his head. When you're trying to persuade someone else to do something, you have to listen to them. This first step is about doing your research and setting the table.

I taught you how to identify someone's behaviour for a reason. This is the time to use it. Where possible try to get a feel for the behaviour of the person you're communicating with, are they Red, Yellow, Green or Blue? Taking the time to try and identify this in the early stages means you will have a better understanding of how their brain works and how to approach them. Chances are that if you're fairly close with the person, you would have already detected their behaviour when reading the previous sections.

In this instance, I am going to say that Nigel is a Blue/Red behaviour blend and Helen is a mix of Yellow/Red behaviours. By acknowledging this, Helen already knows that if she blurts out about moving in together from nowhere, Nigel will just think it's another idea she hasn't given much thought to. She can already see how she needs to adapt her approach to meet Nigel in the middle.

It might seem odd, but to get what you want you have to figure out what the other person wants. Why? Because ultimately we are all the centre of our own universe, if they can't see what's it in for them, they won't be interested. This might sound a little harsh but it's true. Let me explain using the *Titanic.* Imagine you were on the *Titanic* alone with no friends and no family on board. When the ship hit the iceberg, the first person you would want to save is yourself. The fight or flight response kicks in and ultimately it doesn't matter who else is on the sinking ship, you will do whatever you can to ensure there is a space for you on that life raft.

In my opinion, as humans we are hardwired to put ourselves first, it's a survival instinct. That doesn't mean we are all selfish, it just means that even when you help someone, there is always something in it for you, even if it's just the little spark of gratification. That's why when you are trying to persuade someone to do something you want, you can't simply say 'I want this', you have to explain how it benefits them. A lot of people don't do this, instead they only talk about themselves and then question why they never seem to get what they want.

Finally, you need to set the table. If you turn up at dinner and see there are two forks, two knives and a spoon above the plate, you know you're having a three-course meal. Setting the table like this means everyone knows what's going on, they are all on the same page. This is exactly the same as when trying to persuade someone. If Helen corners Nigel and tries to have a conversation with him while he's halfway up the ladder cleaning the upstairs windows, she's on a hiding to nothing. This is the mistake a lot of people make. When there is a tricky conversation to be had, they try to trap someone into a discussion rather than setting the table and giving them space, which is a lot more effective. Remember, timing is everything. What Helen should do is approach Nigel earlier in the week and lay out her plan, for example she could say something like this:

'I was thinking on Friday, while the kids aren't here we could have a nice dinner, I would like to get your thoughts on my leasing situation and talk about something that could potentially make our lives a lot easier.'

Helen knows Nigel is Red like her, so she cuts straight to the point, laying out her plans for the evening and what she wants to discuss; by adding the last part about how it gives them ease of life, she has already piqued his interest. Keep in mind the behaviour of the person you're trying to sell to; if they are a Green you might need to be more subtle, but ultimately it's about focusing on the purpose and explaining the 'what's in it for them'.

Pick one of your 'WE thing' goals and use the table below to understand the potential colours of who is involved in helping you achieve your goals. In the left-hand column write who is involved in your 'WE thing' goal. In the right column jot down their potential dominant behaviour. There might only be one other person involved or it could be more. It doesn't matter how big or small their potential involvement, write their name below and what you think their dominant colour might be based on what you know about them.

This should take you 5-10 minutes to complete.

Who Is Involved?	What Is Their Dominant Behaviour Colour?

Questions

This second step is exactly the same as when you are convincing yourself to take action, except you need to ask the other person the questions. The aim is to always reach a win-win, it should never be one-sided. To do this you need to figure out what they want and need. I am evangelical about questioning techniques, I consider it to be one of, if not the most important part of the whole SMASH IT! method. When you ask the right questions you can learn a lot about someone. This really helps to strengthen the relationship, and as you know, teamwork makes the dream work.

At this point you know what you want but you don't necessarily know how this helps the other person. It's your job to play detective and work out where the middle ground is. How can you help them get what they want? What is the win-win?

There are four key question types that can be used to do this. In the 'ME thing', we focused purely on the open questions, again these are the most important as they will provide you with the most information, however you should be aware of the other question types, how they can be used and also interpreted.

1. **Open Questions** - These are the ones that begin with who, what, when, where, why and how. They are still your most powerful weapon at this stage of the process, as they will help you gain more information about the other person/people involved in making your goal happen than any other question type.
2. **Closed Questions** - These are questions that can only be answered with a yes or a no. They don't necessarily provide you with lots of information but are great to use when you want to confirm you've understood someone's point or reiterate something.
3. **Leading Questions** - This is when you put the answer in the question, for example, 'You have enjoyed reading this book, haven't you?' These are similar to closed questions in that they don't really tell you anything because they kind of force the recipient to give you the answer you want. Again they

can be useful in checking your understanding or you could use them when closing – we will get to this – but you have to be careful because they can be seen as manipulating, which I am sure you can agree is never a good thing.

4. **Rhetorical questions** - These are usually used when you don't actually want a direct answer but rather make a point or say something for dramatic effect. I would try to stay clear of these as they won't help you move any further forward. In fact, they'll usually take you backwards as they come off as being passive-aggressive, often resulting in arguments. For example, when you want someone to help you and they don't do it in a timely fashion, you might say, 'I'll just do it myself then, shall I?'

There is a time and a place for all the question types. However, my advice is to use open questions as much as you can, these are the ones that will give you the upper hand and bring you closer to getting what you want.

Let me expand further why I am evangelical about open questions. In *Secrets of Successful Sales*, I told you how I used open questions to bag six complimentary business class return flights to Australia between Christmas and New Year. You remember this, don't you? No, well you better get your copy and have a read (see, this is a leading question). Now, let me tell you about the time I secured a VIP capsule for me and my pals on the London Eye at the drop of a hat.

One of my buddies was visiting from North America, therefore I, my Canadian buddy and two others had decided to get together in London and make a day of it. We had spent all morning indulging in a bottomless brunch on a boat on the Thames. We had already well and truly caught up on the ins and outs of life when we decided it was time to show our friend from across the pond the great city of London. What better way to see the city than jumping on the London Eye?

It was late afternoon on a Saturday; if you have ever been to the London Eye, you would know that it's one of the city's most popular tourist destinations. The wait in line was about as long as watching the three *Lord of the Rings* films back to back. Of course, unlike all the other willing and eager tourists, we hadn't pre-booked tickets because we were on a spontaneous impromptu trip. So, how were we going to get on the London Eye and show our buddy a good time without having to wait for what I'm sure would feel like forever and a day?

That's when I come in with my open questions. I marched straight up to the customer service desk and asked to speak to the manager. When the manager arrived I jumped straight in with the open questions and asked, "What is your influencer policy?" The purpose of this question was to try and establish a need for something I knew I could fulfil. When the manager replied and informed me that they make special arrangements for influencers, queue the mini fist-pump. This man had practically just given me the keys to the kingdom. I continued with my questions: "Who do you consider to be an influencer?" "What arrangements do you make for influencers?" and "What do you ask from them in return?"

Let's not forget that I had also read the manager's behaviour and adapted my own. I didn't act brash, playing the diva card, demanding this, that and the other. I can tell you now, that would have got me absolutely nowhere, he was a Yellow/Green and knew all about influence. I was humble, polite and walked the thin line between confident and cocky. When you're making a ballsy move such as the one I did, confidence is key, it is not the time to stumble and falter.

It was at this point I whipped my phone out of my pocket and opened up my social media apps. I showed the manager the Facebook,

Twitter and Instagram accounts of my buddies who all have over 100,000 followers, and built up a case that between us we had quite the online following. This is of course all true, my friends were all influencers and had worked with some big names. That's when I put forward my offer: if my friends and I could skip the queue, we would post some live videos across all of our social media profiles and share with our followers why the London Eye was a must when visiting the city. It was a win-win, we got to have a great time and they got free exposure and endorsements.

It was at this point that we were escorted to the front of the line and put in our very own private VIP capsule. The Yellow in me was in her element! This had surpassed even my expectations; I was just hoping to skip the line, but to have our own capsule and not have to squeeze in with another 20-odd people was amazing! We were living the high life, we had all the room we needed to jump around and take our selfies. And this is what makes me notorious for getting what I want. I used the exact process that I am teaching you now to get what I want to SMASH IT! and make it happen. You can do it too.

Let's bring it back to Helen and Nigel, on Friday night when they are having dinner, here are some of the questions she could ask. Remember it is not an interrogation, it is a conversation; these questions should be thrown in sporadically, not make Nigel feel like he is sitting in the hot seat of a gangster film. You can have a list of questions prepared, but it doesn't necessarily mean you will ask them in that order, it is not a script, your questions should bounce off the other person's response. Here is an example of some open questions Helen could ask Nigel:

- How do you think things are going with us?
- How do you think our current living situation impacts the children?
- How can we create more stability in all of our lives?

- What would be the next step for you?
- What is it you ultimately want from our relationship?
- What do you think I should do with my lease?
- When do you think you'll be ready to take the next step?
- What do you think an ideal relationship looks like?
- What do you think are the main challenges with our current living situation?

Continuing on from the task in the previous section, use the box below to write down some open questions you could ask the person you're trying to persuade to help you achieve your goals. Try to think of at least five questions. Remember to start them with who, what, when, where, why and how.

This should take you 5-10 minutes to complete

My Open Questions Are...

CASE STUDY: MEET SIMON...

The Situation

Simon Crowther is a young businessman and was looking to purchase a new house. If you have gone through this process, you will understand that it is expensive and incredibly stressful. Simon's older sister had bought a house a few years before and informed him that she was able to secure free carpets and have her stamp duty paid. Like most people when buying a new home, Simon wanted to minimise costs as much as possible; after hearing his sister's experience, he was hoping he would be able to secure himself a similar deal.

The Problem

Simon was looking to purchase a house on a popular new housing development. He spoke to his house builder and told them his sister's experience, asking if it would be possible to do something similar. Their response was, "Our houses are like gold dust and sell out at a rapid rate. We don't do any extras for free, we don't need to." This was bad news for Simon as it meant he wouldn't save any money. He had fallen in love with his dream home, but it was going to cost him an arm and a leg to get the same finish he had seen in the shiny show home.

When you buy a house most builders will recommend a mortgage provider and solicitor. However, Simon had friends and family who could do it for him at a 'mates' rate' and would benefit from the commission. Like anyone in his position, he was going to try and save money where he could.

The Win-Win

As an incentive, the developers offered anyone who used their recommended mortgage advisor and solicitor free turf, a garden gate and an outside tap. However, this was of no financial gain to Simon as this was worth less than the professional fees. He was holding out for a better deal.

They then asked Simon, "What do we need to do to get you to use our mortgage advisor?" To which Simon responded, "What can you offer?" The sales team offered Simon built-in appliances in return for using their preferred advisor. Since he wasn't saving any money using his friend, Simon agreed to the offer but insisted he still wanted to use his own solicitor.

A couple of days later he received a call from a different member of the sales team. They wanted to know why he had chosen their advisor but not their recommended solicitor. Again he explained the financial motive behind his decision. The person on the phone said, "The thing is our performance is measured on whether or not you use our mortgage advisor **and** solicitor." Simon said this is the point where he knew he had them over a barrel and if he played his cards right knew he would be able to get exactly what he wanted.

After negotiating back and forth, Simon managed to secure himself over £6,000 of additional extras, including the garden turf, gate and tap, built-in appliances, luxury carpets, kitchen and bathroom tiles.

Both parties got what they wanted. The builders wanted to provide quality customer service whilst hitting their performance targets and Simon wanted to save as much money as he could whilst buying his new house and still get the high-end finish. It was a win-win.

The Techniques

Simon followed the process to the letter. The two things that he did outstandingly well were using the open questions and listening to the answers.

Simon asked the housebuilder, “What can you offer?” This is a great open question to start negotiations and get the ball rolling. By doing this he took control of the sale. Although Simon was technically the customer, he identified the opportunity for negotiation and almost turned the tables so that he was in the position of power. When asking open questions, it is equally important to listen. This is something Simon did particularly well; by listening to the builders he managed to gain the important piece of information: performance was measured on customers using **both** the recommended service providers. That gave him the edge to get the best deal. This shows that whether you're the person selling or the person buying, when you follow the process you can always get what YOU want.

Simon's story is the perfect example of what all transactions should be – a win-win for both sides.

Reassure

This step is all about showing the person you are trying to persuade that you really are listening to them and care what they have to say. Any relationship, whether it be business or personal, will not last if you are not genuine and do not care about the other person. Remember this is one of the most important steps when speaking to a relationship-focused person. The process of persuasion is here to help you get what you want, but as I have said before it should be a win-win. When you are trying to work with someone else it is never going to work if you don't take the time to listen to what they have to say. This is even more the case in personal relationships than anything else.

As I have already mentioned, actions can speak louder than words. When it comes to reassurance it isn't about opening your mouth, it's about keeping it shut and listening. Of course you can tell them you understand what they are saying and can see where they are coming from, but don't butt in. Let them speak and use your body language to show them you are engaged and listening. Making eye contact, nodding your head and open posture are all non-verbal ways of showing you are actively listening.

You can also use some small verbal comments like 'yes', 'uh huh' and 'mmhm'. They tell the speaker you are listening without having to cut in and stop them in their tracks. A lot of people only listen so they know when it's their turn to speak, turning the conversation into 'defend' and 'attack' mode, reverting back to the 'Ah… but'. When you're trying to get what you want, you need to actively listen to what the other person is saying and think about what these words mean.

When you're having these important discussions, put the electronics away. Remove as many distractions as you can. If you're both looking around the room or at your phone screens, then neither one of you will feel heard and understood. There is nothing worse than someone scrolling through their phone, giving feedback cues like 'mmhm' and 'yep' and then 10 minutes later asking a question about something you had just told them. It can be infuriating. Please, please, if you're going to put time and effort into following the process and asking the open questions, listen to the response.

I know that this can be particularly hard for certain behaviour types. The more extroverted behaviours like Red and Yellow will struggle not to jump in and have their say. The Reds always want to cut to the chase and the Yellows get excited about sharing their thoughts and ideas. Greens and Blues on the other hand are in their element when it comes to listening. Both Helen and Nigel are Red, so might be fighting to get their words in. However, Nigel is also a Blue and Helen needs to remember this, she really needs to use her body language to show Nigel that she is actively listening and not just talk over him.

I told you that asking open questions was the most important part, but if you're not going to listen then what is the point? Questions give you information, information is knowledge, and knowledge is power.

Thinking back to our question types, this is a good time to use closed questions. You can repeat back what you heard and ask to confirm whether this is correct. For example, Helen might say this to Nigel: 'I see, you think that Harry would benefit from having more structure around our living arrangement, is that right?' By doing this, you are showing that you have listed and understood, thus reassuring them that you really do value what they have to say.

Benefits

This step in the SMASH IT! method is exactly the same as when you are convincing yourself to smash your own goals. Someone will not invest their time with you based on features alone, they need to understand how it benefits them. It goes back to what I was saying about the *Titanic*, in their world it's all about them. The benefits need to be personal, what works for one person won't work for another; when you're outlining the benefits of your offer it needs to be relevant to what the other person wants. Remember, help them to help you. Let's recap on the difference between a feature and a benefit.

Feature *- A distinctive attribute or aspect of something*

Benefit *- An advantage or profit gained from something*

This principle is simple yet something the majority of people miss. You will struggle to persuade on features alone, remember features tell, benefits sell. The biggest offenders when it comes to breaking this rule are those who work in electronic retailers – shhh, don't tell Matt! I'm not sure about you but when I go to buy a new laptop, I have absolutely no idea what it means when they list the features like Intel Core i3 processor, 8gb RAM and retina display. The overload of technical jargon confuses me. However, if they told me that all of these things means the laptop will operate at a high speed and enable me to edit video content, making me look like Audrey Hepburn in *Breakfast at Tiffany's,* well then they've got my attention. The technical language is great when the customer is a techie, but if like me they're just the average Jo, then explaining the features alone will not have them chomping at the bit to hand over their hard-earned cash. They need to explain why those features will benefit me and meet my needs if they want to chalk me down as another happy customer.

I am going to walk you through how to do this using Helen and Nigel. It always starts with the need. If you asked your open questions and listened, you should have a pretty good idea of what the other person's ideal outcome from the situation is. Let's follow one of Helen's open questions and see how she can match up the benefits to Nigel's needs.

Helen: What do you think are the main challenges with our current living situation?

Nigel: It's confusing for the children, Harry doesn't know if he is coming or going most of the time. Between my place, yours and his mum's, he never knows where he is going to be. A number of times he has got to school and realised he has left his sports kit at the wrong house and then had to use the lost property, which he absolutely hates. I do worry that all this shuffling from one place to another is having a negative impact on him.

Helen: I agree, what do you think we can do to provide Harry with more stability?

Nigel: Ultimately I think it would help to stay in one place for longer and ensure that he has a clearer schedule of where he is going to be and when.

From this example, you can see how Helen has used the open questions to dig deeper into Nigel's concerns and reveal the problem. That way she can swoop in with her idea to move in together and offer it as a solution. Now I will show you how Helen can match the benefits to Nigel's needs in order to persuade him to move in with her.

Example A:

Helen: I think we should move in together, I'm nearly 40 and I want to get settled. Plus it would save us both money and means we could take the kids away on a nice holiday in the summer.

Nigel: I didn't realise we were having financial difficulties.

Example B:

Helen: I think we should move in together. Harry is clearly suffering from all the toing and froing, as are Zoe and Tom. If we all live under one roof, at least they would know that when they are with us, they are always in the same place and don't have to worry about packing their bags and forgetting sports kits. It would create more stability for all of us.

Nigel: That does sound like a good idea, definitely something we should consider.

Can you see the difference between the two examples? In example A, Helen has focused more on why moving in would benefit her than anyone else. She has outlined the benefit of saving money, but this was never a concern for Nigel, she has not listened to his responses to her open questions. Helen has assumed that Nigel is thinking about the financial impact of living together, but she doesn't really know if that's the case at all. If she wants to know his opinion on the financial aspect of the situation, then she should have brought it up when asking her open questions. As the saying goes, assuming makes an ass out of you and me. Helen's assumption is disconnected from what is important to Nigel, therefore his response is short and snappy because he feels like he isn't being listened to.

Whereas in example B, Helen has matched the benefit of moving in together to Nigel's needs based on what she discovered from playing detective and asking questions. Nigel's response is much more positive when Helen's idea corresponds to what he said previously; this is because it helps him solve one of his own problems and get what he wants – his son Harry to have stability. That's why even when you are explaining the benefits to someone, it needs to be the correct one that resonates with them. Who knows, by the end of the conversation Nigel might even think moving in together was all his idea!

Have a think about what your goal is and what you're trying to persuade someone to do. What are the potential benefits of them helping you? When you're going through this process in real life, you should of course ensure that the benefits are specific to the person you're speaking with, but for the purpose of this exercise, list in the box below as many potential benefits as you can.

This should take 5-10 minutes to complete.

The Benefits Of Helping Me Get What I Want Are...

Close

The close is the part of the process when you ask for what you want, the thing that you set as your SMART goal. When it comes to getting people to agree to their goals, a lot of people struggle. No matter what they try, they can't seem to get it over the line. The real problem is they haven't actually opened. The thing is, getting somebody to cooperate with you is like a door. You can't close it until it's been opened. What do I mean by opening? Well, that is everything you've done in the process so far, asking good questions, actively listening and selling the benefits. If you've done all the steps correctly, then this bit will be easier.

Most people think the negotiations start after you've gone in for the close but that's wrong, the negotiations actually start before. You should have an idea in your head of what you want to achieve. I always set a gold, silver and bronze deal in my head. The gold is the dream outcome, you almost think achieving this would be too good to be true. Silver is what you would be happy to take, it's a fair deal for you and the other person. Bronze is the lowest you would be willing to go, anything less than this and you would walk away because the deal isn't worth taking.

Let's revisit my complimentary trip of a lifetime to Australia, I briefly mentioned this earlier when I told you about questioning techniques. As you know, Neil and I got married in Jamaica and when we were due to fly back for our wedding reception with all our family and friends, our flight got delayed for 36 hours. This meant that when we finally arrived back home we had missed the best part of our wedding reception and our guests had well and truly started the party without us. We had written to the airline customer service team to complain but they hadn't got back to us, so I did what I do best and I picked up the phone.

Whilst on the phone I requested to speak to the CEO, I didn't quite get that far but I did get put through to the CEO's personal assistant. I noticed her behaviours almost instantly when she started apologising. She was a Green. I told the lady my experience and how Neil and I had missed our own wedding reception. I followed this very process and used the open questions until I went in for the kill. In my head I knew what I wanted to achieve before I even picked up the phone, I had my gold, silver and bronze tiers laid out very clearly:

- Gold - Two complimentary business class flights to Australia
- Silver - Two complimentary economy class flights to Australia
- Bronze - Two complimentary economy class flights to Jamaica

I had this in my head the whole time I was on the phone. I really wanted to take Neil to my old stomping ground in Australia, however I knew this was a long shot. I figured the least they could do was offer us two complimentary flights to Jamaica since this is where we were when we got delayed. However, what I actually secured was six complimentary business class flights to Australia between Christmas and New Year. This had surpassed even my expectations. I only achieved this because I had the gold, silver and bronze ideals in my head; had I not had this I probably would have settled for the first offer I was presented with which was just two economy class flights.

In this instance, I was the customer and able to negotiate on what she had offered. However, as the person working with others to get what you want, my advice is to always start high, you can always negotiate down but very rarely can you negotiate up.

Let's take a closer look at this from the perspective of Helen and Nigel. Helen's big goal is to have a new life partner by the age of 40, the lease on her house is coming to an end and she would like to move in with her boyfriend Nigel. If Helen was to set a gold, silver and bronze for what she wants to achieve, it would look a little like this:

- Gold - Nigel loves the idea and asks Helen to move in straight away
- Silver - Nigel agrees that moving in together is the next step but wants to wait three months
- Bronze - Nigel thinks they should wait another six months until they have been together for a year before they move in together

What are your gold, silver and bronze tiers? Where are you willing to negotiate and at what point would you be willing to walk away? Write next to each tier in the box your corresponding wants. Use Helen's tiers to help you.

Gold (The Best Possible Outcome)

____

____

____

Silver (The Realistic Outcome)

____

____

____

Bronze (The Very Least I Would Accept)

____

____

____

Now that Helen knows where she is willing to negotiate, she can go in for the close. Let's recap on the different types of closing techniques and look at how Helen can use them to win over Nigel and get what she wants.

1. **Assumptive Close** - Remember, this is the ballsy method, you are assuming that you're going to get your way. If you've successfully opened then this shouldn't be a problem, but if you haven't, then a bit like Helen in example A, you will make an ass out of yourself. Let's follow on from example B and say that Helen and Nigel are on the same page; here's an example assumptive close Helen could use: 'Fantastic, I'm glad you think it's a great idea too, when do you think we should get the ball rolling?' She has passed the buck back to him using an open question, from his answer she will be able to see where he sits on her gold, silver and bronze scale.

2. **Alternative Close** - This is still presumptive but gives the other person more flexibility. By giving them two choices, it helps them feel more in control of the situation which will ultimately help get them on your side. The two choices Helen would give Nigel would coincide with her gold and silver levels. For example, Helen could say something similar to this if she was trying to use this technique on Nigel: 'When do you think we should move in together, we could go for it now while my lease is up, or we can wait for three months and I'll renew my lease?'

3. **Worst-case/best-case scenario** - I didn't tell you about this closing technique before but I think it's worth mentioning here. A bit like Ronseal, this technique does what it says on the tin. You close by giving someone the best case and worst case scenario of the situation to try and convince them that whether things work out or not, there is no real loss. If Helen were to use this with Nigel, it might sound a bit

like this: 'Worst case scenario, we move in together for six months, it doesn't work out and I'll look for a new place; best case scenario, the kids absolutely love it and we make it a permanent thing, how does that sound?'

4. **Fear Close** - This is a tricky one to get right. The important thing to remember when using this technique is to always tell the truth and not to use it as a way to manipulate someone else. For example, Helen could say: 'If you're not ready to move in then I can't see a future together.' If Helen were to say this, then she needs to follow through on her promise; if she's not ready to walk away, she should steer clear of using this technique. There is a time and place for using this method; if you use it incorrectly you could risk ruining your relationship and push yourself further away from getting what you want.

The closing method you use depends on the situation and the person you're speaking to. It's your job as the person doing the persuading to analyse the environment and choose the closing type that fits. There is a time and a place for each technique, the fear close in particular. It's really important to take into account someone's behaviour at this point. The fear close doesn't work as well on introverts as it does on extroverts, in the same way the alternative close won't work well with relationship-focused behaviours who struggle to make decisions at the best of times, let alone when they are given multiple options.

Use the box below to practise each one of the closing techniques in relation to what you're trying to achieve from the conversation. As in the 'ME thing', write next to each of the closing techniques your closing line. Then read through them and highlight the one that you think would be most applicable in your situation based on what you're trying to achieve, who you're talking to, and what you feel comfortable with.

This should take you 5-10 minutes to complete.

My Closing Lines Are

____

____

____

Assumptive Close

____

____

____

Alternative Close

____

____

____

Best Case/Worst Case

____

____

____

Fear Close

____

____

____

As you work through the Process of Persuasion, the person you are trying to persuade is transitioning through their own process, I call this the Winning Journey. Why, you ask? Because when the two processes flow together that is when you achieve a win-win. This table below shows how the steps of the Winning Journey fit within the Process of Persuasion in an ideal situation.

Process of Persuasion	The Winning Journey
1. Stop, Look and Listen	1. I'm Interested
2. Questions	2. Tell Me More
3. Reassures	3. You Get Me
4. Benefits	4. I Like What I'm Hearing
	5. We're a Match
5. Close	6. I Want This

Let me break down what each stage of the Winning Journey means. I will use Helen and Nigel as an example to help me explain.

1. **I'm Interested** - Helen gained Nigel's interest in the early stages when she set the table and hinted to the idea of what she wanted to discuss and how she thinks it could benefit both of them. The idea that Helen wants to discuss something that could be of benefit to Nigel piques his interest and he is intrigued to find out more, even if at this point it's just out of curiosity.

2. **Tell Me More** - During the questioning stage, Helen would have asked Nigel lots of open questions to try and get to the root of what he wants from their relationship, hoping to find that he wants the same things as her. During this time, Nigel would have started asking questions back, this is a

good sign as it shows he is interested in what Helen is saying and wants to know more.

3. **You Get Me** - This happens during the reassurance stage. Helen has made the conscious effort to listen to Nigel and this in turn makes him feel understood. Nigel feels like Helen understands his needs and what he wants from the relationship, this gives him confidence to pursue the conversation further.
4. **I Like What I'm Hearing** - This is the point where Helen would have matched the benefits of moving in together to what Nigel wants, explaining how by living together they could provide more stability for their children. This is what Nigel wants and therefore is beginning to come round to Helen's way of thinking.
5. **We're a Match** - Again this happens as Helen explains the benefits of living together to Nigel. He is reassured that their goals and values align and can see that Helen is the person he is supposed to be with.
6. **I Want This** - If Helen followed the process, when she goes in for the close Nigel will jump at the chance to live together and ask her to move in straight away.

This is the ideal situation, when the two processes run parallel it's a win-win, everyone gets what they want.

Deal or No Deal

Wouldn't it be great if you got what you want, first time, every time? Unfortunately, this isn't always the case. There will be lots of times when you go in for the close and you think you've absolutely nailed it; you've followed the SMASH IT! method to the letter and you've got it in the bag. You're just about to throw out a mini fist pump when things take a turn. It's at this point that the other person usually turns around and says, "Oh, I'm not sure about that." To which you're thinking how can they not be sure, I followed the process, they were lapping it up, what went wrong? Well, let me tell you. The likelihood is that you tried to get them on board too soon, this means that while you were working your way through the process you forgot that the other person is on a journey all of their own. The two processes were out of sync and whilst you thought they were ready for the close they were actually still at the Tell Me More stage.

Don't worry, all is not lost. This mistake happens to the best of us and can be rectified. The SMASH IT! method is a circle for a reason: if you get to the end and things haven't gone your way, you just work your way round again. OK, maybe you can skip a step, the important thing is to go back to the questioning techniques. Go back to your open questions and dig deeper; if this was Helen and Nigel, Helen could ask:

- What is it you're not sure about?
- What were you hoping for?
- What would your ideal time frame be?
- What does your idea of living together look like?
- What would be a good solution for you?
- How do you think we could move this forward?

You then need to work your way back round the process but remember to listen, **really listen** to what the other person is saying and try to figure out where they are in their journey. If Helen is going through the benefits of living together and Nigel is still asking questions about logistics, then Helen has moved too fast. If you listen to the other person you will be able to work out what stage they are at and this in turn will help you work your way through the SMASH IT! method and minimise the risk of trying to convince them too soon.

When someone turns you down, they usually want to spare your feelings so will use some sort of an excuse. Imagine you're out and about when you bump into an old classmate. Out of politeness you stop and have a friendly chat, they then suggest you meet up for a drink on Friday evening and hang out. However, you're not really interested in meeting up with them, you only stopped to be polite, you're not going to turn around and say, "No thanks, I don't feel the need to spend more time with you," that would be harsh and you don't want to hurt their feelings. Instead, you fob them off and say something like, "I'm busy on Friday but another time maybe, anyway nice seeing you again." Then you turn around and walk away. You palm them off without actually having to give a straight 'no'.

This is something we all do, not because we want to lie but sometimes it's easier than having to tell someone the truth and risk upsetting them. This is what is called a false objection. The problem is we all do this so much that we no longer know when someone is telling the truth or fobbing us off. Because, of course, sometimes you might bump into an old school pal and really want to hang out with them at the pub on Friday, but you actually do have other plans that can't be rearranged. This is what's called a true objection. If this is the case, then the problem is easily solved by suggesting another day.

In this example, trying to figure out whether it is a true or false objection is easy, but that's not always the case. In fact, a lot of the time it can be really hard to figure out the difference. Put your detective hat on and go back to questioning techniques. It is always about asking the right questions, this is where you will gain the information you need to decide whether it is a true or false objection. This is when you need to play Kenny Rogers, "You've got to know when to hold 'em, know when to fold 'em, know when to walk away, and know when to run." If it's a true objection, then hold in there, you will find a way to make it a win-win, but if it's a false objection and they really aren't interested, then be prepared to walk away. You need to work out if it's a deal or no deal.

Let's run through what this might look like with Helen and Nigel.

True Objection

In this example I will show you how Helen can use the open question techniques to identify that Nigel's objection is true, then how she can follow the SMASH IT! method to overcome this and reach a win-win. You will also see how when dealing with objections that Helen has to rethink about her gold, silver and bronze ideals in order to negotiate and meet Nigel in the middle.

Helen: You think moving in together is a great idea, me too. My lease is up in a couple of weeks, I am ready when you are. When would you like to get the ball rolling?

Nigel: Oh, well I think it's a good idea but I'm not sure now is the right time.

Helen: OK, when do you think is the right time?

Nigel: I'm not really sure, it all feels a bit rushed, we've only been together six months, maybe it is too soon to be taking such a big step.

Helen: What do you think the main concerns would be?

Nigel: You know I've been through all this before with my ex-wife, I've only just managed to get myself sorted after she left, I'm worried that you would move in, it wouldn't work out and then we would both be stuck under one roof. I can't do that, I can't let Harry be around that kind of environment again.

Helen: I understand where you're coming from, I went through a lot with Gary too and I don't want to go through that again, but this is different, neither of us are our ex-partners. We both want the best for our children and that means providing them with as much stability as possible, right?

Nigel: Yes, you're right. Making sure Harry has the best I can give him has always been top of my list.

Helen: How about this: I can extend my lease for a bit, and we can either give it three months and have another chat, or we can wait for another six months as we would have been together for a year and then take the leap? How does that sound?

Nigel: If you're OK with waiting for our one-year anniversary then I would really appreciate it. I know you're eager to move in now, but I just don't want to make any rash decisions after last time.

Helen: Of course not, I completely understand, we have both been through a lot.

Nigel: Thank you for being so understanding, I know that when you do move in it will feel right for both of us.

As you can see, Helen has followed the process to work out if Nigel's objection was true or false. When she realised it was a true objection and the real reason behind it, she could see room for negotiation, which is when she went back to her gold, silver and bronze tiers. She had already gone for gold, so she knew that was off the cards, she delivered the silver and bronze options using an alternative close and managed to reach a win-win with Nigel. She was always prepared to wait six months to move in but she knew she had to try for gold and silver just in case she could make it happen quicker.

False Objection

Going back to what I said about people being afraid to tell you the truth, I am now going to show you how the situation would have played out had Nigel's objection been false. You will see how Helen uses the same questioning techniques to detect the nature of Nigel's objections, but this time she doesn't continue with the process as she realises it's a no deal and she isn't going to get what she wants.

Helen: You think moving in together is a great idea, me too. My lease is up in a couple of weeks, I am ready when you are. When would you like to get the ball rolling?

Nigel: Oh, well I think it's a good idea but I'm not sure now is the right time.

Helen: OK, when do you think is the right time?

Nigel: Hmm, I'm not really sure, it's always hard to tell with these things.

Helen: OK, well what is it about moving in together that concerns you?

Nigel: I'm just not sure it would work; I've only been living on my own for a short time and think it's good for me and Harry. I think changing our living situation again would be confusing for him. We're getting used to it being the two of us.

Helen: I understand, in that case, what do you see as being the next step in our relationship?

Nigel: To be honest, I am quite happy as we are, other than Harry forgetting his sports kit, I can't see there is any real reason that we need to change anything.

Helen: I see, so how long would you be happy to continue as we are?

Nigel: I don't know, I guess until things feel like they need changing.

Helen: OK, just to clarify, you'd be happy if this time next year everything was exactly the same?

Nigel: Yes, things are good as they are, I can't see any reason to change them.

Helen: OK, well I think we are on two different pages.

It's at this point that Helen has to make a decision whether to walk away from the relationship or remain in it. After all, Helen's goal is to find a new life partner. If she decided that she was happy living in that way, she would need to revisit her SMART goals and change the criteria. I know that this is a very basic example and real-life relationships are much more complicated, but whatever your goal is, if it's a 'WE thing' you and the person involved need to be on the same page. If your goals are too different, you will never find a win-win.

In the SMART section, we discussed the two conflicting goals of buying the house in Shepherd's Bush and working part-time. This was a clash of goals and it's the same here. If Nigel's goal is to stay living alone with Harry and Helen's goal is to move in together, they're never going to be able to make that work. If Helen stayed with Nigel in this instance because she thinks she can change his mind, she'll get a year down the line, nothing will have changed, and she'll end up resenting him and their whole relationship. When you're working with someone on a 'WE thing' their goal might not be the exact same as yours but there has to be some commonality which means you BOTH get what YOU want from the partnership. If it's one-sided, it will never work.

In the words of The Rolling Stones: "You can't always get what you want"... well not first time anyway. When something doesn't go right the first time and people walk away from a partnership, whether it be a romantic relationship, job, or big purchase (like a house or a car), the thought of giving it another go can be daunting. People tend to fail once and then fear doing it ever again, like me with the big wave, it's a typical cliché of commitment issues that we see in all the rom-coms. It would be easy for Helen to leave Nigel and avoid getting in a serious relationship for as long as possible in case it doesn't work again, but at least when she tries, she stands a good chance of hitting her goals. If she never tries, her chances of getting what she really wants is zero.

Bringing it back to the esteem section of Maslow's Hierarchy of Needs, I still think that self-love and high self-esteem plays a huge part in getting what you want, especially when it comes to building relationships with others. If Helen doesn't value herself, she won't believe that she is worth more than somebody who doesn't want to move in with her, therefore won't reach her goal of finding a new life partner. It is likely that without knowing her self-worth, she will never fulfil that goal because she will settle for Nigel, living in an endless cycle of what-ifs.

I think this comes back to metathesiophobia, the fear of change. Most people don't trust that the grass can be greener on the other side, they're afraid to make a change. I'm not saying that Helen would be making a mistake to stay with Nigel; after all, you will more than likely have to compromise to a certain extent on some of your goals, but without valuing yourself, you accept whatever is handed to you because you think you couldn't do better.

With the effects of the COVID-19 pandemic looming over the economy as I write this, it's clear to see that 2021 is seeing a drop in the job market. As a result of the global crisis, more people than ever are looking for alternative positions. Does one of your goals relate to your employment situation? I'm sure it does, because like in the Banks of Balance, we all need to feed the bank of cash. Be it securing a promotion or bagging yourself a new job, this method works in *exactly* the same way when it comes to selling yourself to an employer. So, if this is what YOU want, don't be afraid to use it.

Deal or no deal, if you really want something, whether it be a 'ME thing' or a 'WE thing', you are the only person that can make it happen. Don't let a knockback stop you, get out there, be brave and try again and again until you get it. If someone doesn't want to help you reach your goal, find another person that will. As a buddy of mine once said, a no isn't forever, it's just for now. When I set a goal, nothing can stop me. It doesn't matter how many times I get rejected or how many hurdles I trip over along the way, I always keep on going because my goals are SMART, my WHY is strong and I have a growth mindset. You can have anything YOU want, if you follow the steps I have laid out for you in this book. You can SMASH IT!

CASE STUDY: MEET MOIRA...

The Situation

Moira is a 50-year-old mum of two grown-up children, working in the financial sector for the NHS. She is the only one in her household that drives. Like most of us she relies on her car as her main form of transport to get her to and from work, not only that but her husband and son also rely on her to run them around. She is also responsible for her elderly parents and does their shopping for them every week. Moira's car was parked outside her house when it was involved in a no-fault car accident and was deemed a non-economical repair. Moira needs a vehicle if she is going to get everyone to work and keep the household ticking over; what she wants from this situation is to strike the best possible deal with the insurance company to ensure she is financially compensated.

The Problem

Anyone who has been involved in a car accident knows not only how stressful the situation is but how shocking it can be. Even if you're not actually in the car when the accident happens, the realisation that you no longer have a vehicle can turn your life upside down and hit you like a bombshell. Moira needs the car like she needs oxygen. She cannot get to work without it and she can't work from home, this realisation sent her thoughts spiralling into a world of panic. How was I going to get to work? How am I going to afford another car? What if I lose my job? How is everyone else going to get to work? What if we all lose our jobs? Who's going to pay our bills?

Once she had calmed down, Moira realised that it wasn't the end of the world and held hope that her insurance would be able to help her out. After all, that is what it's for. She went through all the boring processes that you do when being involved in an accident. An engineer was sent out to assess the damage of her car and deemed it a non-economical repair, meaning the cost of fixing the car outweighed its worth. Following the inspection, the insurers told Moira they would only pay her £1,995; instantly Moira's hopes were dashed, there was no way she could buy a similar car of the same quality for that price and she didn't have the extra money to fork out.

The Win-Win

Prior to the accident, Moira had been reading my first book. She remembered reading the negotiation section and decided to put the method to the test.

"I remember reading the line in Alison's book, you can always negotiate down, but you can never negotiate up, when the insurers were trying to pressurise me into taking the first offer. I knew that it would be a massive mistake because I wouldn't be able to go back and try to get more after already accepting. I knew I needed time to think and research, so managed to buy myself some time."

She started out by conducting some of her own research into

the value of the car, comparing similar makes, models and specifications. After much research, the cheapest price she could find in the whole of the UK was £3,495 and that was 600 miles away on the other side of the country. She then went to her local garage and got an estimate for what it would cost to make the vehicle both drivable and presentable. She was quoted an all-in price of £500. This was a far cry from the insurer's estimated damage costs of £6,500.

The next step was to call the insurer and question them. "I wrote down a list of open questions that I could use to help negotiate before I called them, without this I think I would have stumbled and got nervous." These were Moira's questions:

- How did you come to the valuation of the car?
- Why do you think your valuation is different from my research?
- How would I go about arranging my own repairs?
- How does that affect the amount you will pay out?
- What is the next step in the process?
- What is the time frame to receive the payment?
- Why is there a difference between the two repair figures?

After pointing out the difference in valuations and questioning their methods and how they can justify the difference between the two figures, the insurers agreed to review the original valuation. Again, throughout the call Moira was feeling pressured by the insurers to accept the offer, she knew the reason for this was the need for them to close her case. However, she wasn't going to let that stop her from getting what she wanted and pushed on with her open questions.

Finally, a few days later the insurance company phoned back and reported, after considering what she had said, they could provide her with a final offer of £2,980. This was an additional £985 more than their original offer and stood her in good stead to purchase another car, which meant she could get back to life as she knew it. "Before reading Alison's book, I would have been too scared to negotiate because I didn't know how, but her process made it seem easy and gave me the confidence to stand up and get myself a better deal."

Why is this a win-win? Well, Moira got almost 50% more than she would have got had she taken the first offer and the insurance company got to close the case and won themselves another happy customer.

The Techniques

The first thing that I have to commend Moira for is staying strong and not bowing down to the pressure and taking the first offer. Most people fall at this first hurdle because they are too scared to negotiate in case they fail. If this is the case for you, do what Moira did, buy yourself some time to think over your options and do your research, that way you will feel a lot more confident when you pick the phone back up.

The second thing that Moira did which helped her case was ask the open questions; questioning their system and justification behind the valuation was a particularly good move. Knowing how the other person (or company in this instance) operates will always help you, as you can then mould your research around it. When it comes to negotiation, I will always tell you to go back to using your open questions because this is where you can gain the most knowledge. Remember, knowledge is power.

YOU CAN SMASH IT!

Shhhhhhh, I want to tell you a BIG secret! Like I said in the beginning, people used my debut book, *Secrets of Successful Sales*, in their everyday lives to get what they want. As I mentioned at the start of this book, I feel it has called me to write it to help people like you to get what YOU want. The truth is, lots of people *hate* sales, but it's not actually sales they hate, it's the fear of rejection that they are scared of. But whether it is a 'ME thing' or a 'WE thing', whether it's getting your kid to do their homework, or convincing yourself to put on your trainers to go for a run, everything we do is a sale! If you can converse, you can convince, which by the way is sales!

As I said earlier, people have used my methods to give them the confidence to do things they only ever dreamed of, like securing a promotion, new careers and life pathways, resolve conflict with family or friends, improve their work-life balance, better deals when buying a house, more money when selling a car, losing weight and organising their finances – this was all based on my teachings from *Secrets of Successful Sales.* Can you now understand why I wrote this book? I can't wait to see what YOU do with everything I have taught you in this book.

Every day you wake up and you have a choice. It can be a good day or a bad day. A goal-smashing day or a goal-dashing day. You are the only one who can make that decision, no one else can do it for you. If you want something, if you really really want it, you're going to have to get up every morning and fight for it. You picked this book up for a reason, I have given you every tool, tip, process and method that I possibly can to set your best foot forward. Now it's over to you. As this book comes to an end, you have two choices:

1) You go out into the big wide world, make your dreams come true, and get what YOU want!

   OR

2) You close this book and pick up another, hoping it will be the one that holds all the magical answers.

So how do you SMASH IT!? Hopefully as you have worked your way through this book, you now have a clear understanding of how you can achieve your goals, but here is a little recap:

1. 8% of people achieve their goals. 92% of people don't. You have a choice of which side of the statistic that you fall into. You now have the tools to get what YOU want; the decision is yours.
2. Stop comparing yourself to other people, it will only drag you down. This is your life, it's all about YOU!
3. Look at the things you can't achieve and turn them into cans! It's a great place to start from.
4. Keep your goals visual and don't let the thief of time distract you from getting what YOU want.

5. Know your WHY. When your WHY is strong, it's hard to go wrong.
6. Work out if it's a 'ME thing' or a 'WE thing'. You can't always achieve your goals on your own, sometimes you need to collaborate to get what YOU want.
7. Think like Tom Hanks in *Cast Away*, sometimes things happen that are out of your control. What is in your control is how you react to them.
8. Awareness of behaviours is crucial. Treat people the way they want to be treated, not how you want to be treated! They will work with you to achieve your goals.
9. Think like Kenny Rogers "…know when to hold 'em, know when to fold 'em, know when to walk away, and know when to run." Know your self-worth. Leaving a goal when it is unachievable is almost as powerful as setting it in the first place.
10. Use the SMASH IT! model, we know it works. Now it's your turn.

What are you going to do? I've said it once before and I'll say it again, this isn't the enchanting world of Harry Potter, there is no magic here, only hard work and determination.

You see, personal development is a bit like sport. You can understand all of the rules of tennis, but it won't make you Andy Murray or Serena Williams when you step on to the court. Nope, there's only one thing that will do that, and it's called practice! That's what you have to do next, take everything you have learned from this book and practice, practice, practice.

So, I'll ask you one last time: are you going to sit there and do the same things you've always done, or are you going to SMASH IT!?

THE CO-CONSPIRATOR

Dyslexia - *a general term for disorders that involve difficulty in learning to read, write or interpret words, letters, and other symbols, but that do not affect general intelligence.*

As a dyslexic author, amazing thoughts and ideas flow through my mind all day, every day but capturing them on paper is like trying to catch a butterfly in a net with no gauze.

To achieve great things you need help, this book would *never* have happened without my friend and kick-ass co-conspirator Kiya Newnham.

Kiya started working for me straight from graduating Bath Spa university at the tender age of 21. Her contributions to my business have not only helped make it the success it is today but have made the journey much more enjoyable.

Travel broadens the mind and I always encourage people to see as much of the world as they can, so I was proud when Kiya decided to spread her wings and open her passport to a new world of adventure.

After several false starts at writing *SMASH IT! The Art of Getting What YOU Want*, Kiya offered to come back and help me catch the butterfly and get the words which were sloshing around my head down on paper. Kiya helped me take something which was a rough idea and turn it into the book that you hold in your hands today. She spent hours researching and adding proven theories, writing up my personal stories and case study examples and editing content to turn it into an easy to follow, fun, comprehensive methodology. I cannot thank her enough for her dedication and passion throughout the entire writing process. You really are SMASHING IT

ACKNOWLEDGEMENTS

Running a business is tough at any time, let alone when you are writing a book alongside the day-to-day tasks. Without the commitment of Rebecca Dobson, my amazing marketing and operations manager who took up the slack in the business to allow me the time to write the book, it may never have happened. Not to mention the final week of edits when we were on Zoom for what felt like 24 hours a day! A huge THANK YOU for all her input and hard work.

Another one of my little birds who has flown the nest to discover the world is Natasha Baer. Natasha is one of the most tenacious people I have ever met, and her bravery and commitment astound me. Thank you for always being in my corner even from the other side of the world. You are The Queen of Grammar and Spelling and decoder of my dyslexic words.

Thank you to everyone who has given their time to tell me their stories of how they used *Secrets of Successful Sales* to enhance their lives and get what they want. Your incredible achievement proves what I teach works and has given me the strength and determination to write this book to inspire others to follow in your footsteps.

It has been a pleasure to partner again with Mindy Gibbins-Klein and her team at Panoma Press to take this from an idea to a book which will change lives. Thank you for all your hard work, support and patience.

And, of course, Neil, Kieran and Connor who keep my feet on the ground and remind me when the dishwasher needs to be emptied or the washing machine needs to be filled!

REFERENCES

Beck Institute. (2020). *History of Cognitive Behaviour Therapy*. [online] Available at: https://beckinstitute.org/about-beck/history-of-cognitive-therapy/ [Accessed 19 January 2021].

Brooks, C. M. (1975). *The life and contributions of Walter Bradford Cannon 1871-1945: his influence on the development of physiology in the twentieth century*. New York: State Univ. Of New York Downstate Medical Center.

Doran, G. T. (1981). *There's a S.M.A.R.T. Way to Write Management's Goals and Objectives*, Management Review, Vol. 70, Issue 11, pp. 35-36.

Dweck, C. (2017). *Mindset - Changing the way you think to fulfil your potential*. Updated edition. London: Robinson.

Dweck, C. (n.d.). *The power of believing that you can improve*. [online] www.ted.com. Available at: https://www.ted.com/talks/carol_dweck_the_power_of_believing_that_you_can_improve?language=en [Accessed 8 April 2020].

Edgar, A. (2018). *Secrets of Successful Sales*. London: Panoma Press.

Spranger, E. and John, P. (1966). *Types of men: the psychology and ethics of personality*. New York; London: Johnson Reprint Corporation.

EISENHOWER. (2016). *Introducing the Eisenhower Matrix*. [online] Available at: https://www.eisenhower.me/eisenhower-matrix/ [Accessed 19 January 2021].

Ensize. (2019a). *Introduction to Puzzle Disc*. Unpublished.

Ensize. (2019b). *Driving Forces*. Unpublished.

Festinger, L. (1954). *A theory of social comparison processes*. Human Relations: The first 10 years, 1947–1956, Volume 7, Issue 2, pp. 117-140.

Good, C., Aronson, J. and Inzlicht, M. (2003). *Improving adolescents' standardized test performance: An intervention to reduce the effects of stereotype threat*. Journal of Applied Developmental Psychology, 24(6), pp. 645-662.

Harvard Health. (2018). *Understanding the stress response*. [online] Available at: https://www.health.harvard.edu/staying-healthy/understanding-the-stress-response. [Accessed 19 March 2020].

HuffPost. (2017). *The Top 10 Things People Want In Life But Can't Seem To Get* | HuffPost. [online] Available at: https://www.huffpost.com/entry/the-top-10-things-people-_2_b_9564982?guce [Accessed 6 February 2020].

Kubler-Ross, E. (2014). *On Death and Dying: What the Dying Have to Teach Doctors, Nurses, Clergy & Their Own Families (50th Anniversary Edition)*. New York: Scribner.

Luhrmann, B. (1999). *Everybody's Free (To Wear Sunscreen).* [online] EMI Records. Available at: <https://www.youtube.com/watch?v=sTJ7AzBIJoI> [Accessed 19 January 2021].

Maslow, A. H. (1943). *A theory of human motivation.* Psychological Review, 50(4), pp. 370-96.

Maslow, A. H. (1954). *Motivation and personality.* New York: Harper and Row.

Maslow, A. H. (1987). *Motivation and personality* (3rd ed.). Delhi, India: Pearson Education.

NHS Blood and Transplant. (unknown). *How Your Body Replaces Blood.* [online] Available at: https://www.blood.co.uk/the-donation-process/after-your-donation/how-your-body-replaces-blood/ [Accessed 19 January 2021].

Office for National Statistics. (2019). *Divorces in England and Wales in: 2018.* [online] Available at: https://www.ons.gov.uk/peoplepopulationandcommunity/birthsdeathsandmarriages/divorce/bulletins/divorcesinenglandandwales/2018 [Accessed 19 January 2021].

Peters, S. (2013). *The chimp paradox: the mind management program to help you achieve success, confidence, and happiness.* New York: Jeremy P. Tarcher/Penguin.

Pritchard, G. (2020). *The myth of meritocracy.* [online] Available at: https://yorkshirebylines.co.uk/the-myth-of-meritocracy/ [Accessed 13 Aug. 2020].

Psychologist World. (Unknown). *Stress: Fight or Flight Response.* [online] Available at: https://www.psychologistworld.com/stress/fight-or-flight-response [Accessed 19 March 2020].

Schwantes, M. (2018). *Science Says Only 8 Percent of People Actually Achieve Their Goals. Here Are 7 Things They Do Differently.* [online] Inc.com. Available at: https://www.inc.com/marcel-schwantes/science-says-only-8-percent-of-people-actually-achieve-their-goals-here-are-7-things-they-do-differently.html [Accessed 13 Aug. 2020].

Simply Psychology. (2020). *Maslow's Hierarchy of Needs* | Simply Psychology. [online] Available at: https://www.simplypsychology.org/maslow.html [Accessed March 2020].

Tierney, J. (2020). *The Power of Bad: And How to Overcome It.* London: Penguin Books Ltd.

William Moulton Marston. (1928). *Emotions Of Normal People.* Alcester: Read Books.